A GUIDE TO
POSITIVE DISCIPLINE

A GUIDE TO POSITIVE DISCIPLINE

Helping Students Make Responsible Choices

BARBARA KEATING

Former Director of Elementary Programs,
Wichita Public Schools, Wichita, Kansas

MERCEDES PICKERING

Coordinator, Elementary Social Studies,
Wichita Public Schools, Wichita, Kansas

BONNIE SLACK

Teacher, Emerson Open Magnet School,
Wichita, Kansas

JUDITH WHITE

Coordinator, Elementary Language Arts
Wichita Public Schools, Wichita, Kansas

ALLYN AND BACON
Boston London Sydney Toronto

Library of Congress Cataloging-in-Publication Data

A guide to positive discipline : helping students make responsible
    choices / Barbara Keating . . . [et al.].
        p. cm.
    ISBN 0-205-12152-7
    1. Students—Conduct of life—Study and teaching. 2. Classroom
management. 3. Decision-making. I. Keating, Barbara, 1927–
LB3609.G84   1990
371.1'024—dc20   89-15122
                                                                      CIP

Printed in the United States of America
10 9 8 7 6 5 4 3 2 1   93 92 91 90 89

Contents

Chapter 3   Assessment   47

SECTION II
CLASSROOM DESIGN
67

Chapter 4   Planning for Classroom Implementation   69

SECTION III
ALL-SCHOOL DESIGN
131

Preface

A Guide to Positive Discipline: Helping Students Make Responsible Choices is a guide for educators who wish to implement a discipline system in a classroom or school focused on teaching students self-discipline, appropriate behavior, and decision-making skills. We cannot teach our students how to do the jobs they will work at as adults because we do not know what those jobs will be. We do know, however, that students will have to make decisions and choices no matter what lifestyles or careers they pursue. It is important that those decisions are based on responsible choices that will allow our children to achieve their full potential as human beings. Students need practice in making decisions that are in their own best interest. In a supportive environment, with caring people, self-discipline can develop.

The philosophical base for this program is: *Virtually all students can and will master the skills needed to function appropriately in the school community if given adequate instruction, sufficient time, and support.* This book provides step-by-step plans and support materials for every aspect of implementing a positive discipline program.

Chapters 1 through 3 and the appendix are addressed to all educators. Chapters 4 and 5 are addressed to the teacher who wishes to implement the program in a single classroom. Chapters 6 through 9 are designed to be used by a principal or school leader in utilizing the program school wide. The appendix contains materials in the form of sample lesson plans, self-analysis charts, and other support materials for implementing the program.

The authors gratefully thank and acknowledge colleagues in the Wichita Public Schools and in the Wichita, Kansas, area. Many friends and associates helped develop, use, test, and refine the component parts of this guide. Thanks are also due to family members of the authors, Bob, Vic, and Gary, for their support and encouragement.

ABOUT POSITIVE DISCIPLINE

CHAPTER 1

Introduction

Welcome to Positive Discipline

If you are an educator, you probably spend a considerable amount of time on discipline, which can be a tough part of your job. Perhaps you are frustrated in your search for a new way to create an environment in your classroom or school where students and adults achieve and feel satisfaction. We understand, because we've faced the same situation many times in our own careers in education.

Positive Discipline is based on the philosophical belief that self-discipline can be taught. Self-discipline is defined as the ability to act consistently on decisions that allow individual achievement, rewarding interactions with others, personal safety, and appropriate use of our environment. Almost all educators would agree on the desirability of self-disciplined students. How to match that desirability with reality is the daily concern of all educators who discipline students in schools. Positive Discipline offers a method of teaching appropriate behaviors and wise decision making reinforced by a system of positive recognition and privileges. The responsibility for discipline is shared by the adults in the school, parents, and, most importantly, the students themselves.

This program has a different philosophical orientation from currently prevalent practices that approach the school behavior of students from a controlling point of view. When we want students to learn addition facts, we teach the concept, show the students how to work addition facts, and allow time for practice. We support the students' learning with praise and recognition for successful attempts or, when attempts are unsuccessful, with correction and reteaching. In this same way, students need to be taught the concepts of self-discipline, shown how to be self-disciplined, and then given time to practice. Students need praise and recognition for successful attempts at demonstrating self-discipline and they need to be retaught and/or corrected when attempts at self-discipline are unsuccessful.

By using the Positive Discipline approach, you can realistically look forward to spending less time in the traditional role of enforcer and more time in recognizing students for appropriate decisons and behavior. When a student has a discipline problem, the adult role is one of understanding and support because the student is the one held responsible for his or her behavior.

It is with a real sense of pride that we present Positive Discipline. In our own schools and classrooms this program has brought multiple and often unexpected dividends to teachers, parents, and students. Although no system can guarantee to meet the needs of everyone, Positive Discipline can work for you if you plan carefully and then carefully work your plan. It has worked for us and we believe it can work for you.

How to Get the Most Out of This Guide

This book is written for two audiences: those who wish to implement Positive Discipline in the school as a whole and those who wish to implement the program in a single classroom. *Regardless of your intent*, read Chapters 1 through 3 all the way through. It's important that you understand the Positive Discipline approach and each step of the process before trying to proceed with implementation. Then, those wishing to implement the program in a *single classroom should read Chapters 4 and 5 and the appendix*. Those wishing to implement an *all-school plan should read Chapters 6 through 9 and the appendix*. We have provided some practical suggestions for each step of both the all-school and single-classroom approaches. The suggestions are not intended to be all encompassing or needed by everyone. However, we have attempted to provide enough specific ideas to stimulate your own creativity.

Although all rights are reserved, the Reproduction Pages throughout this book may be reproduced or revised for use with this text, provided such reproductions bear the copyright notice. Use this program guide as a handy reference whenever you need to refresh or refocus your efforts.

THE POSITIVE DISCIPLINE PHILOSOPHY

Virtually all students can and will master the skills needed to function appropriately in the school community if given adequate instruction, sufficient time, and support.

Positive Discipline is based on the belief that virtually all students can be taught to make appropriate decisions that support their own well-being and the well-being of others almost all the time. The program builds on this philosophy by helping the school staff provide direct instruction in the skills students need to make appropriate decisions about individual achievement, interactions with others, safety, and surroundings. Behavioral expectations are developed and then explained, taught, and practiced. Students are taught about the decisions or choices they make each day that impact their lives in the school. They are taught how appropriate choices will help them successfully achieve, interact with others, remain personally safe, and care for our environment.

Successful attempts at making appropriate decisions and choices are followed by positive consequences, including recognition and privileges. These are balanced by reteaching and/or planning and using logical (rather than punitive) consequences when students make unwise choices that affect their own and others' well-being. Clear expectations and consequences guide students in their decisions as they learn the skills needed for life-long success. Within this structured framework, a climate is built that fosters students' growth in self-discipline and personal responsibility.

Underlying Research

The Positive Discipline program is based on formal research conducted on discipline during the past fifteen years and supported by the authors' practical experience with successful discipline in classrooms and schools.

An effective discipline program is based on systematic instruction designed to teach students self-discipline and responsibility. A discipline program is most effective when it includes a teaching process focused on stimulating appropriate socialization and preventing problems, rather than on enforcement, control, and compliance. Students must be seen as willing and potentially cooperative but needing guidance, instruction, support, and time for practice.

In 1985, the Cline/Fay Institute distributed a series of letters, *Principally Speaking*. The notion was expressed that affording children choices and holding them responsible for their decisions is a real-life practical approach to preparing children for the lifetime of decision making that is the essence of daily life for adults. In the issue "Special Thoughts on Raising Kids," the subject of decision making is addressed.

According to the Institute, whether at home or at school, mistakes are often better teachers than lectures. As adults, our choices about disciplining children play a significant role in the development of future skills in children's decision making. The Institute maintains that attempting to impose control on children only seems to help adults satisfy unconscious needs to feel more adequate as adults. Demanding to get our own way only teaches youngsters to be stubborn and demanding themselves. Providing opportunities for making appropriate choices followed by logical consequences is a way to help children learn to become responsible decision makers and adults in a very real world.[1]

Researchers have contributed significantly to the body of knowledge about discipline, but practical research that can be applied to actual classroom and school situations has surfaced only relatively recently. The Mid-Continent Regional Educational Laboratory (McRel) compiled much of the research in a document entitled *Discipline*.[2] In this document, certain characteristics of effective schools, teachers, and classrooms were identified as factors contributing to effective school discipline. Many of those characteristics support the Positive Discipline philosophy and approach:

School Characteristics
- Students are involved in making school rules.
- School rules are clear, positive, and stated in behavioral terms.
- Rules are enforced consistently.
- Students are expected to succeed at following school rules.
- Rules are taught with the same care, clarity, and priority used to teach subject-area lessons and students are provided opportunities to learn, practice, and be successful.
- The focus is on rewarding rather than punishing behaviors.

Teacher Characteristics
- Problem-solving activities are used that avoid win-lose conflicts.
- Teachers are consistent in what they say and do.
- Follow-through on commitments is evident.
- Students are treated with respect and courtesy.
- High expectations are held for all students.
- Students understand the consequences of behavior.

- Group closeness is promoted by arranging for cooperative activities, by discouraging competitive cliques, and by being careful not to show favoritism.
- Teachers are knowledgeable about the special characteristics of the various cultures.

Classroom Characteristics

- Problems are prevented by teaching and demonstrating classroom rules and procedures at the beginning of the school year then allowing time for students to practice.
- Classroom rules are consistent with school rules.
- All areas of the classroom are scanned frequently and the teacher knows what is happening in all areas of the room.
- Students are taught survival skills such as how and when to listen to the teacher, follow directions, or ask for help.
- Students are provided frequent, specific, positive feedback on both academic work and behavior.
- Personal and social skills are taught through lessons on conversing, listening, helping, and sharing.
- Well-planned lessons with materials prepared in advance are taught using a brisk and appropriate pace so students stay on task.
- Long periods of delay and confusion are avoided by using smooth, brief transitions between lessons and activities.

McRel's review of discipline referenced Donald Cruickshank, Jere Brophy, Walter Doyle, Thomas Good, Carolyn Evertson, Edmund Emmer, Jane Stallings, Joyce Putnam, Thomas Lasley, and William Warpon among others.

According to Emmer and Evertson, the first three weeks of school appears to be the critical time for teachers to establish high academic engagement rates and low rates of off-task behavior by students. They advocate this be done by teaching pupils to behave appropriately and by shaping behavior with a variety of rewards and signals.[3]

C. M. Charles, in *Building Classroom Discipline, From Models to Practice*, recommends staff training in the actual practice of intervening and following through on misbehavior. He advocates demonstration, participant practice, corrective feedback, and coaching. Other critical elements of staff training, according to Charles, include teaching techniques for controlling misbehavior, encouraging positive behavior, building student/teacher relationships, enlisting parent support, and moving toward self-discipline with a preventive, supportive, and corrective program. He believes students need to be aware of the logical consequences for choosing to misbehave. Charles stresses a built-in system for monitoring and reviewing the function of a discipline system.[4]

The authors believe some critical characteristics of principals should also be considered in regard to effective discipline.

- Classrooms are monitored frequently.
- Encouraging notes and comments are provided to students and teachers.
- Both working hard and playing hard are promoted.
- Recognition is provided for success.
- The positive growth of student behaviors is monitored by helping teachers see, nurture, and positively recognize student growth.
- The principal is involved with students in positive ways.
- The principal works with teachers to provide suggestions and plans to promote appropriate student behaviors.

Although some of the research is couched in terms that reflect the current prevalent "controlling" approach to disciplining students, it has guided the authors as they have developed their approach to discipline. Positive Discipline incorporates research in a systematic way that allows the application of principles of effective discipline. The focus, however, is on teaching, not on controlling. A lesson plan model is used to enhance the teaching process and step-by-step materials provide support. This is not a program that *guarantees* success, however. No written program can do the complex job required to foster effective citizenry. In the final analysis, a sound, caring, effective discipline program depends primarily on truly committed, educational professionals and on continuous, persistent analysis and study with constant monitoring and revision. You, as one of those professionals, will use this guide in your own way, according to your personal philosophy of discipline, in partnership with your faculty, students, and community.

Endnotes

1. Cline/Fay Institute, "Special Thoughts on Raising Kids." *Principally Speaking* (Delta, CO: Cline/Fay Institute, Inc., 1985).
2. C. L. Hutchins, Susan Everson, Robert Ewy, Susan Lynch, Lawrence Mello, Barbara Kessler, and Linda Shalaway, *Discipline* (Kansas City, MO: Mid-Continent Regional Educational Laboratory, 1983).
3. Edmund T. Emmer, Carolyn M. Evertson, and Linda M. Anderson, "Effective Classroom Management at the Beginning of the School Year," *Elementary School Journal*, 80 (1980): 218–228.
4. C. M. Charles, *Building Classroom Discipline, From Models to Practice*, 2nd ed. (New York: Longman Inc., 1985).

Suggested Readings

Anderson, L., and Prawat, R., "Responsibility in the Classroom: A Synthesis of Research on Teaching Self-Control," *Educational Leadership, 40* (1983): 62–66.

Duke, Daniel L., and Jones, Vernon F., "What Can Schools Do to Foster Student Responsibility?" *Theory Into Practice, 24,* no. 4 (1985): 277–285.

Jones, V., and Jones, L., *Comprehensive Classroom Management* (Boston, MA: Allyn and Bacon, 1985).

Kounin, J., *Discipline and Group Management in Classrooms* (New York: Holt, Rinehart and Winston, 1970).

Lasley, Thomas J., and Warpon, William W., "Characteristics of Schools with Good Discipline," *Educational Leadership* (December 1982): 28–31.

Madsen, Charles H., and Madsen, Clifford K., *Teaching Discipline: A Positive Approach for Educational Development,* 2nd ed. (Boston: Allyn and Bacon, 1974).

Wayson, W., and Lawley, T., "Climates for Excellence: Schools that Foster Self-discipline," *Phi Delta Kappan, 65* (1984): 419–421.

Wolfgang, Charles H., and Glickman, Carl D., *Solving Discipline Problems: Strategies for Classroom Teachers,* 2nd ed. (Boston: Allyn and Bacon, 1986).

CHAPTER 2

The Positive Discipline Program

Rationale

Discipline has been and always will be an important part of life in our schools. It is a common thread running across generations. It knows no language barriers. Anyone who takes a serious look at our society today will recognize the need for change in the approach to discipline in our schools. Our courts and our prisons are full of people whose self-discipline failed them.

One only needs to pick up a newspaper to find examples of young people, and indeed our national leaders, who find themselves in painful circumstances because of decisions. In Wichita, Kansas, during the spring of 1988, three college students were involved in an assault for which prison terms resulted. If these students had been given chances to practice the skill of considering choices before acting, perhaps painful consequences could have been avoided.

A study of our court systems today shows vast backlogs of case loads for judges. Yet, in more and more cases true criminal intent is just not present. Instead, poor decisions make criminals out of previously law-abiding people. Young adults sometimes find themselves in serious trouble due to one unwise decision.

Decision making seems to be an area where life suddenly gives us a test without time to practice or study our decisions. Without previous practice in decision making and in experiencing the consequences of choices, young people can fail a decision test that can influence the quality of the remainder of their lives.

Schools are being called upon more and more to provide skills that help children avoid devastating decisions. Across our nation, programs are being mandated in areas such as drug education, AIDS education, law-related curriculum, and personal safety. The following lists indicate a close match between the goals of these major topics that are impacting teaching time today and the primary goal of Positive Discipline—wise decision making.

Drug Education Programs

1. *Community Based:* Involves parents, medical professionals, law-enforcement personnel, and school personnel.
2. *Teaching Methods:* Requires active student participation, including discussions, simulations, role playing, and writing.
3. *Focus:* Understanding, accepting, and behaving consistently with a core set of cultural values and development of a positive self-concept.
4. *Skills Taught:* A universal set of skills needed for healthy living, including thinking skills, decision-making skills, communication skills, interpersonal skills, and so on.

Human Sexuality Education Programs

1. *Community Based:* Involves parents, medical professionals, law-enforcement personnel, school officials, and other personnel.
2. *Teaching Methods:* Requires active student participation, including discussions, simulations, moral dilemmas, role playing, writing, and so on.
3. *Focus:* Understanding, accepting, and behaving consistently with a core set of cultural values and development of a positive self-concept.
4. *Skills Taught:* A universal set of skills needed for healthy living, including thinking skills, decision-making skills, communication skills, interpersonal skills, and so on.

Law-Related Education Programs

1. *Community Based:* Involves parents, medical professionals, law-enforcement personnel, school officials, and other personnel.
2. *Teaching Methods:* Requires active student participation, including discussions, mock trials, simulations, moral dilemmas, role playing, writing, and so on.
3. *Focus:* Understanding and valuing the need for law and a system of justice.
4. *Skills Taught:* A universal set of skills needed for active citizenship, including thinking skills, decision-making skills, communication skills, interpersonal skills, and so on.

The Positive Discipline Program

1. *Community Based:* Involves students, parents, and all school personnel.
2. *Teaching Methods:* Requires active student participation and involvement in determining expectations, consequences, and privileges through discussions, role playing, writing, and so on.
3. *Focus:* Understanding, accepting, and behaving consistently with an agreed upon set of standards and development of a positive self-concept.
4. *Skills Taught:* A universal set of skills needed for school and life-long success, including thinking skills, decision-making skills, communication skills, interpersonal skills, and so on.

Our whole American system rests on the premise that "we, the people" ought to have the freedom to make responsible decisions about our own destiny, with a minimum amount of interference and restriction. Freedom works best when practiced by a responsible citizenry, but we find apathy and disregard for personal citizenship almost everywhere. Positive Discipline promotes actually teaching and practicing the skills necessary to help individuals make responsible decisions today and in the future.

Our students will have to make decisions and choices no matter what lifestyles or careers they pursue as adults. Those decisions must be based on responsible choices that will allow them to achieve their full potential as human beings. By providing students practice in making decisions that are in their own best interest, Positive Discipline helps the sense of self-worth grow.

In order for students to know what good decision making is, someone has to *teach* them. They have to be taught appropriate behaviors and how to make wise choices. They have to practice. They have to experience some successes that result in positive consequences, and they have to understand that choosing unwisely and making mistakes also results in consequences. It is much easier to learn while the consequences are only mildly uncomfortable rather than life-crippling.

Positive Discipline is based on the belief that life-long success depends on self-discipline, which can be learned in the school setting. Students develop responsibility for their own behavior and learn to make appropriate decisions about achievement, interactions, safety, and surroundings—four decision-making areas that are explained in detail later.

Positive Discipline can be either an all-school or classroom plan. The support system includes students, teachers, parents, and the principal. It promotes a good school or classroom climate, establishes a positive learning environment, and is based on current research into the characteristics of our most effective schools.

For students, Positive Discipline promotes critical thinking with lessons about making choices, evaluating alternatives, assuming personal responsibility, and solving problems appropriately. It also recognizes student success and provides positive feedback. The approach nurtures personal satisfactions when students make wise decisions and recognizes the powerful role peer support can play in making appropriate choices.

For teachers and staff, Positive Discipline emphasizes prevention instead of punishment, reducing stress levels and putting more enjoyment and teaching into each day. Little record keeping is required, although examples are included for use as needed. Sample lesson plans are provided which can be customized for any classroom situation. A number of suggestions are offered for helping problem students or difficult classes succeed with Positive Discipline.

Positive Discipline helps the educator provide instructional leadership and instruction with a step-by-step implementation guide. The process of defining a Positive Discipline program for your school or classroom will foster teamwork. Because Positive Discipline stresses positive outcomes for students, staff, and parents, cooperation between those groups is usually enhanced.

Step-by-Step to Positive Discipline

The easiest way to understand Positive Discipline is to visualize it as a step-by-step process with several avenues toward success or "feedback loops." Figure 2–1 illustrates the relationship between each step.

Understanding Each Step

Assessment

A needs assessment will help you begin with an understanding of your discipline and behavioral situation today. It gives you an opportunity to find out how everyone perceives the current discipline situation—including the students, parents, and, if you wish to involve an entire school, teachers and other staff members. Surveys, focus groups, and student or staff meetings can be effective methods to gain information and insight into the concerns and perceptions of all the different constituencies within your school and community.

Involve Others

The most important step in building an effective discipline program is convincing others to cooperate and contribute. Successful programs

Figure 2–1. Positive Discipline Flowchart

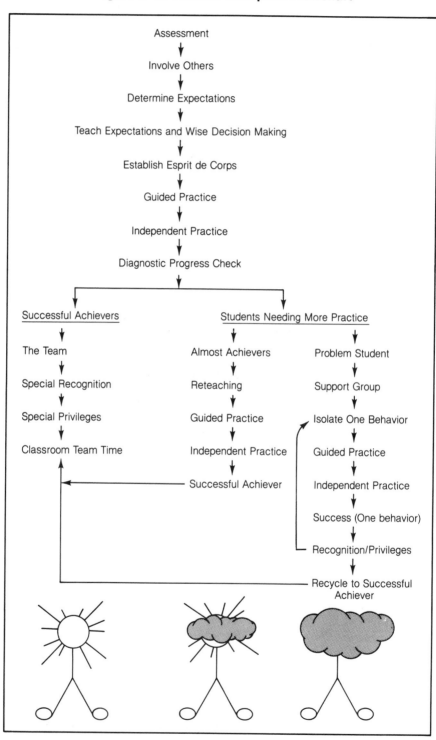

Assessment
↓
Involve Others
↓
Determine Expectations
↓
Teach Expectations and Wise Decision Making
↓
Establish Esprit de Corps
↓
Guided Practice
↓
Independent Practice
↓
Diagnostic Progress Check

Successful Achievers | Students Needing More Practice

Successful Achievers	Almost Achievers	Problem Student
The Team	Almost Achievers	Problem Student
Special Recognition	Reteaching	Support Group
Special Privileges	Guided Practice	Isolate One Behavior
Classroom Team Time	Independent Practice	Guided Practice
	Successful Achiever	Independent Practice
		Success (One behavior)
		Recognition/Privileges
		Recycle to Successful Achiever

don't just happen. They achieve success through leadership and support from everyone involved. Positive Discipline must be explained carefully and thoroughly to those affected by any possible change. As you involve others, emphasize the features that address problems identified in the assessment process. When educators, parents, and students begin to understand the Positive Discipline program, you will be on your way to building a team that will enthusiastically participate in implementation. At first, students will participate because the program is fun and because they like the recognition. Later, they will learn to enjoy and appreciate the feeling of making their own appropriate decisions that are in their own best interest.

Determine Expectations

Expectations are replacements for "the rules." Rules in schools are similar to laws in society. Each year we spend billions of dollars to enforce laws. When we make rules in schools, they need to be consistently enforced. Since we don't usually have police officers in schools, teachers and staff have to take on the enforcer role. Otherwise we are teaching students to ignore the rules (laws) of the adult world. The enforcer role is not pleasant. It is demeaning to staff and students alike. Expectations provide guidelines for personal behavior and decision making.

The classroom is the special domain of the teacher and the students assigned there. Positive Discipline provides considerable flexibility for individual teachers to choose their own methods of classroom management; however, involving students in developing expectations for their own classrooms is stressed. Usually, students who help develop the expectations and understand why they are needed become partners with the teacher in classroom management.

Teachers develop expectations with the students, then the students learn to make choices and decisions based on those general guidelines. Discipline is more effective when stated in terms of expectations rather than rules. Rules have to be constantly monitored and enforced by staff, whereas expectations are monitored by children practicing wise decision making. Walking in the hall is a reasonable expectation, but may be impossible to enforce as a rule since people are not available to monitor the hall constantly. Expected student behaviors must be clearly defined and simply stated. They should be behaviors that can be seen, counted, and measured. Keep expectations to a reasonable number so teaching, learning, and recognition are simplified.

Teach Expectations and Wise Decision Making

Once the school and/or classroom expectations are clearly and positively stated in behavioral terms (seeable, countable, and measurable), the next task is to teach expectations to students with the same care and clarity used to teach content-area lessons. Students are not expected to know words or numbers when they first come to school. Similarly, we should not expect them to know how to behave in school situations, especially in groups of twenty-five to thirty or larger. We should also not assume they know about decision-making processes and how decisions and choices effect consequences.

Establish Esprit de Corps

Some of the skills of self-discipline are social. *Esprit de corps* is a French term meaning "spirit of the group." Group spirit skills are taught by establishing a warm and caring classroom environment and by teaching students how to contribute to that environment by caring for and including each other in activities.

Establishment of esprit de corps is partially dependent on the actions of the teacher. The teacher needs to exhibit an acceptance of each student's presence and innate worth in verbal and nonverbal ways. By paying attention and listening when students are speaking, by calling students by their names, by demonstrating a willingness to help solve problems, the teacher exhibits accepting actions. A nod, smile, wink, or hand signal can acknowledge students' worth in nonverbal communication. Adults can model esprit de corps when interacting with other adults in school settings. Accepting actions can be taught and practiced.

The development of esprit de corps helps students feel good about themselves and encourages their involvement in accomplishing group goals—academic as well as behavioral. Group identity is promoted by arranging for cooperative experiences and by discouraging cliques. When we feel accepted, cared for, and secure, we contribute and work effectively.

Guided Practice

As expected behaviors are learned, teachers carefully guide students' practice attempts by providing the same kind of consistent, positive feedback they give to students as they learn reading and math skills. For example, as students learn about walking quietly to and from classrooms so others are not disturbed, the teacher guides successful practice attempts by smiling at individual students or by making a positive statement to the entire class. This book presents techniques that encourage teachers to focus on consistently recognizing successful attempts at wise decision making rather than punishing students' attempts or lack of attempts to learn the skills and actions of responsibility. Punishment only stops behavior, it does nothing to build desired behavior. When necessary, students are retaught and/or logical rather than punitive consequences for inappropriate behavior are developed. Logical consequences follow as the result of behaviors that are not in the students' best interests. Students are involved in problem-solving activities that help them learn to avoid power struggles and win-lose conflicts. In this way the school setting becomes more like the settings students will deal with as adults. Students learn skills and behaviors to help them cope and survive as effective and responsible adults because they are encouraged to do so in a variety of ways. Extrinsic rewards (external and tangible) are used sparingly. Intrinsic rewards (inner and natural) are the major motivators.

Independent Practice

Guidance is gradually withdrawn as students' skills at being self-disciplined grow. This independent practice period helps to build students' confidence in their newly learned skills and allows them to feel the pleasures and joys that come with being successfully self-disciplined.

Diagnostic Progress Check

Since students are human and therefore far from perfect, teachers continue to provide at least a minimal amount of support as they informally diagnose which students are truly demonstrating consistent self-discipline, which students need more instruction, time, and support, and which few are going to need more instruction, time, and support than the teacher alone can provide. Students are encouraged to assess and analyze their own behavior in order to develop critical thinking and intrinsic motivation.

Successful Achievers

Successful achievers are encouraged to continue to be self-disciplined and responsible with a weekly special activity time called Classroom Team Time and by becoming members of an all-school or classroom club or team. Members are given special privileges and wear some type of special membership symbol during the school day. Almost all people enjoy earning membership in special groups, and students are no exception. The Positive Discipline Team is unusually special because it is a nonexclusive team and all students are expected to become members during the school year. Competition for team membership is discouraged. Students and staff alike help all involved achieve membership.

Students Needing More Practice

Nonachieving students are divided into two subgroups: "almost achievers" and "problem students." The majority of these nonachievers need only a bit more instruction, time, and support from the teacher and classroom group to achieve success. The teacher and the successful achievers work together to provide that support.

Almost Achievers.   Almost Achievers receive some additional instruction, guided practice, time, and support. Then, further independent practice takes place followed by a second diagnostic progress check. Almost Achievers usually move into the ranks of Successful Achievers, and are recognized and awarded privileges.

Problem Students.   A few students will need more than just additional instruction, time, and support from their teacher and classroom group. In these cases, a Support Group is used to augment the classroom group. Other adults and occasionally student friends are identified to provide still more support and encouragement. A specific behavior of the student is identified and addressed with instruction. By focusing efforts on one behavior at a time, a nonachieving student has a real chance at being partially successful. Guided practice is given and partial successes are encouraged and recognized. Independent practice is then again attempted. Success with a single behavior is achieved when that behavior ceases to cause problems for the student. Success breeds success. Another problem behavior is identified and the cycle continues until these students also become self-disciplined and responsible achievers.

Positive Discipline focuses on stimulating appropriate socialization and on preventing problems. Instruction, followed by acknowledging appropriate behavior with a variety of recognition and privileges, is used as the formula for success. Throughout, students are seen as willing, potentially capable and cooperative, but needing guidance, instruction, support, and time for practice in becoming successful decision makers.

Applications for Middle School

Positive Discipline can also be used successfully with a classroom or school that includes students in fifth grade and above. Since the authors' experience is primarily with students in kindergarten through grade six, and since the program was designed and implemented in two elementary schools, a complete middle school plan is not presented here.

However, additional involvement of students is thought to be critical to the success of the program in upper grades or in a middle school.

Applications for Middle School

Elementary Plan	*Middle School Plan*
Assessment	Assessment involves students.
Involve Others	Students or a group of students are involved in data analysis and in decisions concerning the school or classroom.
Determine Expectations	Students have initial involvement.
Teach Expectations and Wise Decision Making	Students help teach and/or a relaxed, more informal approach to the suggested lesson plan is taken.
Establish Esprit de Corps	Establish esprit de corps in a homeroom or advisor/advisee program during class meetings.
Guided Practice	Students help guide practice.
Independent Practice	Students help with independent practice.
Diagnostic Progress Check	Students assist with progress checks.
Successful Achievers/Students Needing More Practice	Student Senate Forum* is involved.

After the first year, a microworld of responsible citizenry and government can develop. Interested social studies teachers or history teachers would make excellent co-sponsors with the principal in an all-school plan. The program then would be data driven by the desires and needs of diverse groups within a school and could result in a very real world of positive conflict. A practical forum for responsible personal and social resolutions should emerge.

---

* A Student Forum should help decide all aspects of the team, including requirements for team membership, privileges, and activities. The Forum should also help with deciding logical consequences for the classroom or school as a whole. Support groups for problem students could include members of the Student Forum.

Key Concepts

The Positive Discipline program contains several key concepts critical to implementing the philosophy. A discussion of each concept will help you understand the total program. The key concepts are presented here as separate items for further clarification and because you may wish to use them as handouts to orient staff, parents, and/or students.

Key Concept 1
Determining Expectations

In determining expectations for a school or classroom, four decision-making areas are stressed in Positive Discipline: achievement, interactions, safety, and surroundings. In general, making appropriate decisions and choices in these four areas is really what having a happy, productive life is all about.

Some typical decisions we make or have made in the area of *achievement* as adults might include chairing a town committee, going to college, or going to work every day. For children, the decisions could include getting good grades, working hard at school, or perhaps becoming an Eagle Scout.

Interactions is the area that includes how we relate to others and to respecting the rights of others. For adults this could include making appropriate choices about caring for family members, developing and sustaining friendships, and contributing to the community. For children it might involve developing friendships, getting along without fighting, and being respectful of the rights of others.

The *safety* area deals with the decisions and choices we make to keep us physically safe and healthy. Either as children or adults we constantly make decisions where we, hopefully, say no to dangerous or harmful things. Decisions involving our human sexuality and respect for law and order are included in this area. We can choose to eat sensibly and exercise. We drive safely and obey traffic laws. Students need to choose to use playground equipment safely, avoid bodily secretions of others, walk instead of run in the halls, and fasten their seat belts in the car. This is personal citizenship.

The area of *surroundings* involves decision making about the care of our environment. It is citizenship in the group sense. For example, as teachers, we take care of and use AV equipment properly. Children need to decide to take care of their own belongings and school property.

With Positive Discipline, what we expect of and teach students are decision-making skills they will use throughout their lives. If you think about some discipline problems you have recently experienced, every problem will fit into one of the Positive Discipline decision areas.

Key Concept 2
The Teaching Model

The Positive Discipline program uses a structured teaching model (The Teaching Model) drawn from currently popular effective teaching models to develop sample lessons. The lessons found in the appendix are designed to help teach decision-making skills students need to function in school and the adult world. The Teaching Model provides methods to teach lessons on behavior and decision making in the same way we now teach lessons in reading and math. The model can be used at all grade levels and can be easily adapted to fit a particular teaching style. The model contains ten steps, which need not be used sequentially.

Focus. A short activity or statement is given that focuses students' attention on the objective, introduces the lesson, and prepares students for the instruction. For example, a discussion of the Positive Discipline team is used to begin the lesson "Introducing Positive Discipline to Students."

Rationale. A statement that provides students a reason for accomplishing the objective of the lesson is given. The rationale makes the lesson meaningful. For example, a statement is made that it is important to make this the best school year possible.

Objective. A written or verbal statement is presented that tells students exactly what is to be learned (content) and how they will show they have mastered the lesson (behavior). For example, "The student will state four decison-making areas and give an example of a wise choice in each area with 100 percent accuracy."

Input. Activities that provide the information students need to accomplish the objective are presented. For example, the teacher discusses the four decision areas: achievement, interactions, safety, and surroundings.

Model. An example (or examples) of what is expected of students is presented. For example, the teacher gives examples of choices people make in the four decision areas and the resulting consequences. For many students, the model is the critical part of the lesson. It helps students understand what they are to do.

(continued)

Key Concept 2 (*continued*)

Guided Practice. Students are given opportunities to practice the expected behavior with teacher supervision and guidance. For example, the teacher has students talk about choices they have made in each area and the consequences that resulted.

Independent Practice. As students begin to perform the expected behavior, additional practice opportunities are provided with minimal or no direct teacher supervision. For example, the teacher has the students write or draw about choices that result in positive consequences for each area.

Diagnostic Progress Check. Activities allowing the teacher to gather diagnostic information about how well students are learning the objective are provided. For example, the teacher can observe and gather information about students from the students' writings or drawings.

Correctives. Additional and alternative learning activities that provide practice for those students who do not show mastery on the diagnostic progress check are presented. Different methods of teaching the same content must be used. For example, students could be asked to role play responses to situations.

Extensions. Additional learning activities that provide practice at higher levels of thinking for students who have mastered the skills, or an opportunity to work with the objective in a more creative, in-depth way, are provided. For example, students are asked to try to think of decisions or choices that do not fit in one of the four Positive Discipline decision areas.

Key Concept 3
Building Esprit de Corps

Esprit de corps is a French term meaning "spirit of the group." Esprit de corps is present in a group when every member feels cared for and included, and willingly supports efforts toward group goals. In Positive Discipline, the group goal is that all students will make appropriate decisions and choices about their own and others' well being virtually all of the time. To reach that goal, all students must feel cared for and included. Students must support each other's efforts to make appropriate decisions and choices. In essence, with the development of esprit de corps, the classroom becomes much like an effective family unit.

Developing esprit de corps is a key component of the Positive Discipline program. To develop esprit de corps, students must be taught the skills of successful group memberships: how to care for and include others, how to support and approve of efforts made toward the goal of self-discipline, and how to have pride in the accomplishments of the group. In order to develop self-discipline, students need the support and approval of their classmates as they learn appropriate interaction skills. For example, a classroom group might discuss and implement ways to help each other finish lessons on time. This support, coupled with the skills when learned, will help students function well in society all their lives.

Developing esprit de corps can be an especially powerful tool for the classroom teacher. It can help ensure a positive classroom climate. When students learn the skills of helping each other feel cared for and included, there is a decrease in tattling, scuffling, inappropriate language, and name calling. When students are taught to encourage each other to strive for self-discipline and to make wise decisions and choices, the teacher's work is made easier. Developing esprit de corps sets students up for successful interactions and enhanced academic learning.

The following Esprit de Corps Lesson Plans are included in the appendix:

- "Caring for Others"—1: Actions that show caring for others are identified and discussed.
- "Caring for Others"—2: Students identify and practice actions that show caring for others.
- "Including Others": Students identify and illustrate actions that include others in play and work.

(*continued*)

Key Concept 3 (*continued*)

- "Caring for and Including Others": Students identify reasons why everyone in the class needs to feel cared for and included, and they practice caring and including actions.
- "Defining Esprit de Corps": Students define esprit de corps and identify actions that show esprit de corps.
- "Responsibility": Students identify actions that help themselves and others act responsibly and make wise decisions at school.
- "Working Toward a Classroom Goal": Students demonstrate esprit de corps by working toward a classroom goal.
- "Helping Others Feel Worthwhile": Students learn to make and accept positive statements about one another.
- "Analyzing Esprit de Corps": Students describe how they feel about classroom esprit de corps.

Key Concept 4
What to Do When Students Choose Wisely

Teaching behavioral expectations and appropriate decision making is really no different from teaching math or reading. The appendix contains many examples of lessons designed to teach specific expectations and the skills of appropriate decision making. Once the specific concepts and skills are taught, an important aspect of the Positive Discipline program is recognizing students for making appropriate choices and successfully achieving. In the first stages of teaching and learning, immediate, consistent, and frequent positive feedback is essential. We encourage you to engage students in discussing the choices and decisions they make as they learn. For example, "Susan, you are choosing to finish your lesson quickly. Tell us about that decision." "Row 2 has decided to line up quickly and quietly for recess. Good for you. How does that help you?" "Jason, you did a good job this morning coming in and getting ready for the first lesson. Will you tell us why you decided to get ready for the lesson so promptly?"

Most educators know exactly how to support students in the acquisition of specific academic skills. What the authors are encouraging you to do is support the acquisition of behavioral and decision-making skills. At first, you may even wish to provide some concrete, extrinsic rewards such as stickers or small items for students or groups of students exhibiting appropriate behavior and making wise decisions. The goal, however, is to move rapidly from immediate, extrinsic (external and concrete) motivation to delayed recognition and intrinsic (inner and natural) motivation. When students are receiving enough gratification from within to sustain appropriate, long-term behaviors, we have accomplished our long-range objective.

Actions to Provide Consistent Positive Reinforcement

1. Establish eye contact and give a nonverbal positive reinforcer such as a wink, a smile, or a thumbs-up signal.
2. Verbally recognize students who are meeting expectations. For example, "John is ready for directions and so is Sally. They are choosing to behave in ways that help their learning." "Row 1 is working very quietly. They are choosing to get a lot of learning done." Use this technique especially when you are tempted to recognize children for inappropriate behavior.
3. Recognize the students by allowing them to participate and/ or choose activities already planned for the day. For example,

(continued)

Key Concept 4 (*continued*)

"Row 1 worked so quietly, they may line up first for recess."
"Sally, you have done a fine job with that math paper. You choose the first story I am going to read for our class story time today."

4. Classroom Team Time: At the end of each week, consistently set aside a short, specific amount of time for special activities for students who have achieved self-discipline or who are making measurable progress towards self-discipline. Classroom Team Time activities should be varied and "up beat." Select activities from the suggestions provided or have students or small groups select from a teacher-approved list of individual or small-group activities. You may need to make arrangements for those few students who occasionally do not earn Classroom Team Time, possibly sending them to another teacher with appropriate assignments.

Suggested Classroom Team Time Activities

At first, it may be somewhat difficult to think of special activities to use in the classroom for recognition. The following list of suggestions may help spark imaginations. Of course, you use only one or two of these ideas for each Classroom Team Time. The possibilities are unlimited.

Small-Group Activities

- Design and decorate a bulletin board.
- Hold quiet conversations.
- Have a book, comic book, or magazine exchange (parent approval may be needed).
- Organize a music combo and play for the class (family members could be included).
- Set up board games or puzzles in a corner of the room for ongoing use.
- Water paint on the chalkboard (approval from principal/custodian may be needed).
- Run errands or do special chores.

Individual Activities

Ideas followed by an asterisk (*) can also be used as small-group or class activities.

(continued)

Key Concept 4 (*continued*)

- Choose stories or a book to be read orally by a student or the teacher.
- Skip a quiz or a written lesson (design certificates for this).
- Exercise: jump rope, sit-ups, foam ball, and hoop.*
- Teach a new game (indoors or outdoors) to class.
- Have a student create and display a bulletin board about himself or herself for day or week.
- Use headphones to listen to tapes from home.
- Use art materials from the art area.*
- Play computer games (brought from home).
- Keep the classroom mascot on a student's desk or allow a student to take the mascot home for the night.
- Eat munchies.*
- Provide a letter or certificate of recognition to be mailed to a grandparent or a special adult friend.
- Distribute a coupon booklet designed by teacher.
- Bring a musical instrument and play for the class.
- Use a rubber stamp on a student's hand or papers.
- Develop a script using home VCR footage (teacher-approved) and show to the class.*
- Use colored pencils for daily work.
- Design and make buttons using a button-making machine.*
- During lunch time work on a 1000-plus puzzle in the corner of the lunch room.*
- Be written up for the class newspaper.
- Write an article for the school/class newspaper.
- Draw a picture for the school/class newspaper.
- Choose to stay in at lunch time or recess.*
- Help students in another classroom.*
- Wear a name tag or badge.
- Check out the class camera overnight.

Large-Group Activities

- Arrange for a telephone hookup with a famous personality.
- Design a class banner for the classroom door.
- Decorate the classroom door using a theme.
- Design or add to a personal or classroom scrapbook.
- Listen to the radio, records, or tapes (preview may be needed).
- Trade library books, read for three to five minutes, then repeat.

(continued)

Key Concept 4 (*continued*)

- Design and construct individual blowing apparatus and/or blow bubbles out of doors.
- Have an informal time with the principal (including snacks, questions, answers, etc.).
- Have an extra story time with the librarian, principal, or teacher.
- Cook in the classroom.
- Go on a class trip.
- Have class (team) members design quilt blocks. Adults put the quilt together. Display the quilt in the hall for several days or weeks. Raffle or draw a name and award the quilt to a student.
- Eat lunch in the classroom.
- Have an extra recess.
- Recognize students at a special assembly.
- Decorate the classroom door with achievements.
- Be recognized in the school newsletter for an achievement.
- Have visting time with classmates or a special staff member.
- Have a special gum-chewing or candy time.
- Have a picnic.

Key Concept 5
The Team

Belonging to the classroom or school team is the primary recognition and privilege provided to students who are making appropriate decisions and choices about achievement, interactions, safety, and surroundings. The team is a nonexclusive group and everyone is expected to become members. There are many ways to organize the team. It is important that both students and, in the case of an all-school plan, staff are involved in deciding the details of membership, including selecting the team name, determining membership eligibility and privileges, and planning the ceremonies to induct members. Students can be involved through the existing student council or through a small classroom or school group especially selected to discuss ideas and make suggestions to the teacher or the staff.

Tips on Organizing a Team

1. Select a name for the team, perhaps using the school mascot or the school colors. In an all-school plan, the name selected must appeal to all age levels. Some suggestions to get you and your group started include: Royal Knights, Golden Treasure Team, Flying Eagles, Black and Gold Team, Blue Falcons, Lions' Pride, Bear Brigade, and so on.
2. Select a symbol that can be worn by team members. The item will be a signal to all of a significant accomplishment. A contest can be held to design the symbol. Many inexpensive symbols such as buttons, badges, ribbons, or athletic head or wrist bands can be purchased or made. Parent groups are almost always willing to help with the purchase or making of badges or ribbons. Whatever is selected, be sure it is something sturdy since many students will elect to wear the item everyday. Also, be sure to make arrangements for those occasions when students lose the item. Extra team symbols can be purchased and sold at cost to students. Be sure to order or make items well ahead of the first induction ceremony.
3. Purchase extrinsic reward items (optional). Some small token or toy can be given along with the wearable symbol to each new member of the team. Again, parent groups are usually willing to help with expenses. Businesses frequently offer coupons to school groups.
4. Determine the standards for team membership. Several options are possible.

(continued)

Key Concept 5 (*continued*)

a. Option 1—Earn/Maintain: Students are recognized as team members when each individual student together with the classroom teacher decide the student is making appropriate decisions virtually all of the time. Other students become members as they, too, reach the independent level. Once a student becomes a member of the club, membership must not be taken away. It has been earned. Membership privileges can be suspended, for short periods of time, when students behave like the children they are and occasionally act impulsively or unwisely. While membership privileges are temporarily suspended, the teacher reteaches the student and provides both guided and independent practice. Suspension of privileges should be reserved for the most serious cases of unwise decision making. The teacher must work with the student to develop a plan for guided and independent practice. The student surrenders the club symbol to the teacher or principal and the problem and solution are discussed. The symbol is withheld until both the teacher and student agree privileges can be restored.

b. Option 2—Automatic/Maintain: After guided and independent practice, all students become members of the team and must maintain appropriate decision making in order to remain active members who are eligible for privileges. The suspension of membership privileges must not be viewed by students as punishment or rebellion is inevitable. Skillful teachers who involve students in determining eligibility and suspension of membership privileges prevent rebellious behaviors which may include withdrawal or verbal outbursts.

c. Option 3—Partial Membership: Some students demonstrate appropriate decision-making skills at certain times of the school day or when they are with certain teachers. For example, some students might demonstrate eligibility for membership in their classroom, homeroom, or special education room but may have problems during recess. These students can be awarded partial membership and some privileges for their successful times of the day. Later, as success promotes more success, full membership becomes possible.

(*continued*)

Key Concept 5 (*continued*)

5. Determine procedures for the induction ceremonies. Many options are possible. In a single classroom, certificates can be issued to take home to parents, a special bulletin board can be constructed to display memberships, or laminated cards of membership, badges, or ribbons can be issued and a short ceremony can be held.

   In order to preserve student dignity, ceremonies should involve members only. Parents can be informed of membership by letter. Students who do not achieve membership need extra support and can be sent to other areas or classrooms during the inductions. Assure them that they will soon become members. In one school, the authors elected to give teachers small certificates for each student. The teachers issued the certificates to students as they became eligible for team membership. Additional large certificates were sent home to parents. As classroom groups became eligible, students met with the principal for a short induction ceremony. The small certificates were exchanges for badges and the original certificates were posted on a large bulletin board in or near the principal's office. Visitors to the building almost always asked about the posted certificates and they became an excellent public relations tool. The certificates were an easy and convenient record-keeping system.

   A typical ceremony involved four steps:

   a. Students in scheduled classroom groups came to the principal's office.
   b. Certificates were posted.
   c. Badges were awarded with congratulations.
   d. A small concrete reward was also distributed. (The reader should carefully consider the use of concrete rewards.)

6. Determine dates for induction ceremonies. The first ceremony is typically held at the end of the sixth week of program implementation. Subsequent members can be inducted weekly or bi-weekly. When membership reaches 75 percent or more, inductions can be scheduled as needed.
7. Determine team privileges and rewards. Members must be recognized with special privileges. Everyone can be involved in deciding membership privileges. Wearing the badge, button, or ribbon is a daily privilege. In a single classroom, priv-

(*continued*)

Key Concept 5 (*continued*)

ileges and activities such as those mentioned previously in "What to Do When Students Choose Wisely" (Key Concept 4) can be used. In an all-school plan, some typical additional privileges that can be awarded include membership in special groups (Student Council, Red Cross, Patrol, Lunchroom Helpers, Office Proctors, Library Helpers); teacher's aide; peer tutor; no hall pass needed when button is worn; lunches or informal time with the teacher, principal, or special guest; or bulletin board designer/decorator. At regular intervals, rewards such as bookmarks, stickers, or an extra recess can be provided to members. All-school events can be planned for team members such as a gum/candy day, an animal sound contest or a silly contest, hat day, or a special assembly in schools where everyone is involved in implementation.

Key Concept 6
What to Do When Students Choose Unwisely

It is very important to maintain discipline using every possible positive technique at your disposal. Effective use of specific praise statements directed to students choosing appropriately is a powerful tool to stop inappropriate behavior. "Sam got to work quickly!" is the intervention most likely to get Sally to work.

It is just as important to let students know immediately when their choices resulting in misbehavior are not acceptable and will not be tolerated. Generally, *teachers must not ignore or accept misbehavior.* The only time it is appropriate to ignore misbehavior is when a student tries a new misbehavior and it is not being reinforced in any way (by other students, for example).

Every teacher needs a variety of techniques to select from when misbehavior needs to be confronted. The teacher should first select techniques that are relatively nonconfrontive, inconspicuous, and unobtrusive, thereby preserving precious instructional time, student dignity, and teacher energy. Here are some suggestions:

1. Address misbehavior in an inconspicuous and relatively non-confrontive way:
   a. Use proximity control. Walk to where the student is misbehaving.
   b. Use a nonverbal message. Establish eye contact and frown, for example.
   c. Involve and redirect. For example, call on the student to help with a particular task or answer a question.
2. Address the misbehavior directly and as unobtrusively as possible:
   a. Call the student by name and indicate "no" with a nonverbal signal.
   b. Call the student by name and give a hint or ask a question. For example, "Mark, are you choosing wisely?" "Katie, is what you're doing helpful?" "Melissa, you may need to choose more wisely."
   c. Direct the student to stop immediately. For example, say in a quiet, gentle yet firm voice, "Sam, stop that please!" "Jane, please no!"

When misbehavior cannot be corrected by using inconspicuous techniques, it is time to communicate with the student directly

(continued)

Key Concept 6 (*continued*)

and positively. An informational rather than a controlling style should be used. We need to assume that students want to behave and get along. When correction is needed, the desired behavior must be clearly stated as a friendly reminder. Always allow students to explain, if they wish, but do not accept excuses. Hold students accountable for their behavior. Involve students in solving the problem whenever possible and then follow the event with positive recognitions of the student's appropriate behavior. Do this without fail and as soon as possible. The intervention will stop misbehavior, but we want also to build self-discipline.

These typical examples may help clarify the technique of positive, direct communication:

1. State your expectations and state what needs to be done. For example, "Jim, you are not choosing wisely. I expect you to be responsible for your achievement. You can do that by stopping your talking and by letting me see you get to work." "Class, you are not all choosing wisely. I expect you to be responsible for your achievement. You can do that by taking your seats and stopping the visiting when the bell rings." "Carolyn, you are a neat kid, but you are choosing to not be responsible for your own and others learning by talking in the halls. I need to hear no talking in the halls. Are you going to need help with that next time we pass in the halls?" Follow up by watching for desired behaviors and verbally complimenting the student(s) when it occurs.

2. State your expectations. Have the student take some time out to think about choices and behavior. Involve the student in deciding on logical consequences. For example, "You are responsible for getting along with others. You ran right into Sandy. Take some time out to think about what you can do to show Sandy she is cared for and respected. Tell me what you plan to do when you are ready." Follow up by watching for desired behaviors and compliment the student when those behaviors occur.

3. State your expectation. Have the student practice and model the expectation. You will be reteaching the expectation and this will need to be done at a time when the student will want to be doing something else. Arrange for the student to lose a preferred activity or lose a privilege. For example, "Julie, I

(continued)

Key Concept 6 (*continued*)

expect you to be responsible for your own safety and the safety of others. You are having a problem with running into others. This is dangerous. You will need to go sit by yourself and make a plan that will help you remember not to run into others. You may not play with the others until we discuss your plan." This activity may also need to involve the parent and/ or the principal. When Julie is allowed to play with the others, follow up by watching for the desired behavior. Be sure to compliment her for appropriate behavior as soon as possible.

Crisis Situations. Occasionally, student misconduct escalates rapidly into a crisis situation. A crisis situation is a sudden problem that stops learning, teaching, or playing. Temper tantrums and students hitting others are typical crisis situations. Frequently, a crisis will involve more than one student. When this happens, several steps should be followed. First, stop the behavior by intervening with a command or an action. Keep calm. Allow the student or students to cool down. Ask each student to state or write about the problem and how they feel. Insist on a clear statement of what they themselves did, not just what the other person did. Ask, "What did *you* do?" Have each student repeat the other's statement of the problem or have each one read the statement written by the other and then say the same thing in his or her own way. Discuss the problem with the students. Help students develop a plan.

Logical Consequences. When consequences are called for, select a logical consequence and explain the selection with a normal tone of voice rather than a vindictive or "get-even" tone. In her book *Positive Discipline* (Sunrise Press, 1981), Jane Nelsen describes three criteria for determining a logical consequence: "related, reasonable, respectful."

A logical consequence must be directly related to the behavior it is aimed at correcting and it must be readily understood by the student. Deliver each consequence with a tone of regret and avoid any connotation of punishment. You expect the student to take control of his or her own behavior by learning to consider choices before acting. If this can be done, the teacher need not take control of the situation. For example, ask the student who is consistently not ready to go to recess to remain with you when you dismiss the

(continued)

others. Then say, "Tim, I asked you to stay because we usually have to wait for you when its time for recess. I thought if you waited for your recess today to talk with me about this problem, it would help you understand how the other students feel."

The following are some examples of logical consequences of student actions.

Logical Consequences

Student Action	*Examples of Logical Consequences*
Talk without permission.	Explain that time taken from class must be repaid. Have the student repay lost class time at recess.
Run in the hall or talk in the hall loudly.	Explain that some extra practice must be needed to learn this skill. Have the student practice walking and not talking in the hall. The practice could be done at recess.
Shove someone or run into someone.	Have the student take time out to think about the unwise choice and to think of what should have been done.
Call someone a name.	Have the student think of two actions that would help the callee feel better. Offer the student the opportunity to do the two actions but do not force the situation. A true choice is needed in order to build intrinsic motivation.
Choose wisely.	Explain that everyone makes mistakes from time to time. As adults we usually try to correct

(*continued*)

Key Concept 6 (*continued*)

	mistakes or to make up for mistakes. Invite the student to think of ways to correct the mistake or unwise choice.
Argue about who won or lost a game.	Have the student make up lost class time during the next game or miss the next game to think about how to be a good sport.
Disrupt a class.	Have the student take time out to write a plan to improve. This may need to be done with the principal.
Make a mess.	Have the student clean up the mess.
Cut in line or push in line.	Have the student go to the back of the line or stay out of the line with the teacher. The student should line up with the teacher until a verbal plan and commitment to improve is made.

A Case for Avoiding Overreacting. Be mindful of the dignity of students as you apply the concepts of logical consequences. Once in a while a generally well behaved student will choose unwisely. If the student is also a hard worker, is usually trustworthy, and is rarely or never in trouble, you might choose to handle the matter in the following way. First, give the student time to reflect. Discuss other topics such as events in the past. Share personal information about yourself in order to set the stage for communication. Then ask if the student is happy about the way he or she handled the problem. Close with stating your belief that you think you can count on the student to make more appropriate choices in the future.

Key Concept 7
Students Needing More Practice

Almost Achievers

After the classroom diagnostic progress check, the teacher makes the decision about which pupils are Successful Achievers and which still need more guided and independent practice. The teacher continues to work with those whose growth needs only a little more time and support (the Almost Achievers). Almost Achievers are given extra time to achieve success and encouraged to help analyze their success at following expectations. Self-analysis and even more positive recognition for appropriate decisions are usually all that is needed. The appendix contains self-analysis charts for use with students.

One author was frequently accused of inconsistent discipline until everyone on the staff began to understand the Positive Discipline approach. The author was consistently taking action to help students learn and grow. Students were dealt with according to their individual growth patterns, thus, not all students were treated the same.

For example, one day a student got in a fight because someone called his mother a name. The mother was in the hospital because she had attempted to keep her drunken husband from beating the student. The author discovered there was no food in the house and the student had been taking care of three preschoolers all weekend. The student needed time and support, not punishment, and perhaps not even logical consequences. When help with the home crises was received and thinking time was allowed, the student was able to analyze the fighting behavior and plan for more appropriate actions in the future.

The Support Group

Those problem students who are not responding to the problem and/or who have multiple behavior problems are referred to the Support Group. The Support Group can be a lifeline to the teacher. It accepts or shares the major responsibility for student behavioral growth and provides insight and encouragement.

The Positive Discipline program seeks to remain positive by using a Support Group to break the self-defeating failure cycle in which students with behavioral problems sometimes find themselves. Along with having a philosophical belief that virtually all children can be taught to behave appropriately when given ade-

(continued)

Key Concept 7 (*continued*)

quate instruction, time, and support, staff members must also be determined to help every child succeed. The Support Group is an additional way to help students take small steps toward success.

Usually, the principal is the person who accepts the major responsibility for a student's Support Group. The principal helps the student select Support Group members and engages these others in expressing interest in the student's progress from time to time. Persons selected should be "significant others" to the student and may include such people as the Physical Education or Music teacher, the librarian, a former teacher, a counselor, a parent, and occasionally a peer or another student. In the experience of the authors, a child rarely selects a parent for Support Group membership. The selections have included a former teacher or a teacher the student especially admires.

The process to help a troubled student need not be time-consuming for the Support Group leader or members of the group. Suggested activities might include the following: A group leader/ student/teacher conference is held to identify the behaviors that need to be changed. A contract is devised that targets only one behavior at a time on which to work (see page 95). A method for keeping track of and recognizing progress is devised. Other members of the Support Group are selected and informed of the contract. Support Group members check frequently with the student concerning progress and provide support and encouragement. Sometimes a note of support is left in the student's desk.

As the targeted behavior ceases to be a problem for the student, another behavior is selected. Further support and encouragement are provided. When the student satisfactorily completes the necessary cycles of the contract, he or she re-enters the Almost Achiever category and the teacher resumes the responsibility for behavioral growth.

More Information about Working with Problem Students

The goal to have every student achieve full membership is sometimes difficult but extremely worthwhile. The longer a student fails to achieve the necessary success, the more important it is to support him or her.

Each student is unique, but there is always some way to make

(*continued*)

a difference. The authors have tried a variety of techniques that have helped these problem students achieve success. One method is to issue special one-day or half-day citizenship certificates. At the end of the specified time, involve the student in analyzing progress and provide recognition and privileges for the next day for successes.

An Example: A special certificate was pinned to a first-grade girl each morning. The girl's behavior was relatively acceptable during most mornings. At noon, the teacher praised the girl's successes and encouraged her to maintain her wise decision making during the afternoon. The certificate was not issued automatically for the afternoon. During the afternoon, the teacher helped this student analyze her appropriate and inappropriate choices. Soon, an afternoon came that was particularly successful. The following day, the teacher issued the certificate for both the morning and afternoon and stressed that the girl had now earned the certificate for her afternoon decisions.

An Example: One sixth-grade student enjoyed the privilege of calling the principal after arriving home to an empty house and sharing successes of the day. Somehow that privilege was the key to this student's needed support. Slowly, a better citizen began to emerge.

Another technique is to provide special membership for particular school times or areas. For instance, one problem student was an outstanding citizen during physical education but was having a difficult time in all other classes. A special badge was awarded that she wore only during physical education class. Soon, she began to display the same kind of citizenship during music class and was allowed to wear the badge during music. Then she earned the same privilege during the math portion of her regular classroom time. Gradually, she earned full team membership.

Another problem student made excellent behavioral progress in his regular classroom but was not able to demonstrate appropriate behavior outside the classroom and away from the regular classroom teacher. A special badge was issued to be worn during times when he was in the classroom. This measure of success seemed to extend gradually to times when he was out of the classroom. The badge and some extra privileges were then issued as progress began. Gradually, he too earned full team membership.

(*continued*)

Key Concept 7 (*continued*)

A third successful technique is to provide anonymous support. For example, one student who was so lonely, so confused, so burdened with a troubled life was helped by a volunteer staff "secret pal." Since there was little appropriate behavior to be recognized, the staff member slipped encouraging notes in the student's desk and occasionally provided small gifts like an eraser or a braided friendship bracelet. After about a month of anonymous support, the student's disruptive, self-destructive behaviors began to change and a better citizen slowly emerged.

A fourth technique is to be more persistent than the student. For example, during the first year the authors implemented the program one author worked all semester with a student we'll call John. At the beginning, John wouldn't look at or talk to the author, so she began by just talking to him. As she became a little wiser in her own decisions about this student, she started to call for John to come to her office about five minutes before his scheduled recess time. She began these sessions by stating the goal she had in mind for their daily talk. If the goal was reached, John could go to recess. He soon began to miss only one or two minutes of his recess privilege.

One day in early April John was sent to the office by his teacher for disrupting the class with a temper outburst. The author told him she was sorry he had made that choice because she knew he could make better choices. She also warned him that when (not if) he earned his school team membership she was going to hug him and he couldn't stop her. John glared.

However, one lovely day in May he walked into her office and directly into her arms with a wide smile. When they finished hugging and laughing, he said, "You really didn't believe I'd ever get my membership, did you?"

She replied, "I always believed you would. I just had to wait until you told yourself you could."

The story has a sequel. This year the student was a sixth grader. The year was somewhat better, but as one might expect, rocky at times. One day in mid-May John stopped the author in the hall and said, "I've done better this year, haven't I!"

The author assured him he had and asked him what she'd told him the first time he'd earned his team membership. John quoted her exactly, word for word, "You always knew I could. You just had to wait until I told myself I could."

(*continued*)

Key Concept 7 (*continued*)

Two Incidents

Two incidents further illustrate the techniques used when working with problem students.

Incident One: One of the authors was working with a second-grade student who could swear with the very best. These were not your standard four-lettered words, but really foul and colorful expletives. He even had the accent right. Some of his classmates had never heard such choice language. Swearing had to be a part of this student's home environment which was high middle-class suburbia.

When the mother came for a conference, she confirmed that both she and the father used this type of language frequently but since they didn't permit their son to use it, she was surprised to learn that her son's language patterns were causing him problems. Desiring to avoid labeling the behavior as good or bad since the parent's values were being questioned, the situation was illustrated by asking the student to imagine himself taking a bath in church. Giggles promptly followed. That illustration helped establish a common meaning of inappropriate behavior. Everyone bathes, but at appropriate times and in an appropriate setting. The language in question was not appropriate at school.

The conference led to finding appropriate words or ways to respond to anger, frustration, or pain. The student shared additional phrases that were both appropriate and not appropriate. A list of appropriate responses was compiled and the classroom teacher was asked to review the list with the student when needed. A call to his mother was made to ask for further work on appropriate responses for both at home and at school.

Was the child at fault or was the parent? To be angry and punitive to a student may close the door to building appropriate responses to real problems. As of this writing, the language in question still occasionally surfaces; however, the frequency and colorfulness has diminished.

Incident Two: A student left sixth grade after being in our school seven years. As the principal, I knew him well. There was very little we managed to do, beyond giving him a feeling of some success. Sometimes he felt successful for only days at a time. At other times the successful days stretched into a few weeks. When he was a fourth grader, I stopped calling his parents for support.

(*continued*)

Key Concept 7 (*continued*)

The parents were punitive and did not seem to help at all. My continuing message to the student was, "I know you can, when you want to."

His biggest success came when he was in my office for detention one day and he offered to write a computer program to address individual letters for recognizing students' academic achievement. He eventually completed the task.

Two years after he had left our school for junior high school, I received a call. He had won an eighth-grade class award: "Student making the most academic and personal progress."

CHAPTER 3

Assessment

The impetus for changing the approach to discipline in your school or classroom may come from a variety of sources, but your interest in Positive Discipline probably reflects your own dissatisfaction with present conditions or that of a small but very vocal segment of faculty or community. One thing is almost certain: Either at the end of the last school year or at the beginning of the current one, you or someone has said, "We need to do something about discipline!"

So, where do you begin?

Self-Assessment

One way to begin is by evaluating your present discipline program. Divide a piece of paper into two columns, putting the words *Works Well* at the top of the first column and *Problems* at the top of the other column. List your successes on one side and the problem areas on the other. You may want to work on the assessment over several days, adding items as they come to mind or, if school is in session, as you encounter them on a daily basis. After you have developed a representative list of the strengths and weaknesses of your current plan, you are ready to analyze your list and determine areas you wish to change. As you implement Positive Discipline, retain those procedures that work for you and include suggested procedures in bringing about the other changes you desire.

A Self-Assessment is included in this chapter (see page 51) if you wish to use a slightly more formal self-analysis. In any case, it is best to have a clear understanding on paper of the problems before embarking on any change effort.

Group Processes

You need to know as much as you can about the attitudes, feelings, and perceptions of your school populations, so that each of their unique needs will be considered before you make changes. A solution that works well for the teacher but gets the parents upset is not likely to be successful in the long run. A system that you like but makes the students or staff uncomfortable isn't going to foster teamwork and cooperation.

Just talk—and listen! Your first step may just be to get out and talk with people about discipline at your school or in your classroom. You can have informal one-on-one conversations with parents after the next parent meeting. You can meet with your students or staff individually to discuss the subject. Take advantage of any opportunity to ask parents, teachers, staff, and students what they think about discipline, and listen carefully to what they have to say.

Focus Groups

You may want to hold several "focus group" sessions during which you focus a group on the topic of discipline with people from each of your school or community populations. An instructional staff or a parent focus group might include five to ten people brought together for an hour or so just to express their feelings, concerns, and attitudes about the current situation. A student focus group might include students who have either negative or positive leadership qualities and are representative of various ethnic groups and sexes. Leading such a group discussion isn't too difficult. Start with the question: "What do you really think about discipline in our school or in our classroom?" and be prepared to listen and take notes.

Tips on Leading a Focus Group

The purpose of a focus group discussion is to allow the participants to express their feelings, concerns, and attitudes towards a particular situation—in this case, discipline. It is not intended to be very rigidly structured with a set agenda, nor is it designed to be a problem-solving session. The major benefit is allowing the leader to get a clear understanding of the problem and the emotions surrounding it.

When you invite people to attend, clearly state the purpose of the session and the subject to be discussed. Tell them when the session will start and when it will end, including day, date, times, and location. Have a chart board or blackboard handy on which to write key comments. Design a series of questions to stimulate conversation such as, "What do you think about the current discipline situation at our school or in this classroom?" "How do you feel about that?" "Why does inappropriate behavior occur at these times?" and "What do you hear from other parents or students?"

Don't try to "lead" the group or make a lot of statements yourself— you're mostly there to ask questions, keep the discussion going, and listen. At the end of the session, thank everyone for participating and explain how their comments will be used (e.g.: "Thanks for sharing some of your thoughts today. I appreciate your openness. Your comments will help me understand the situation better and will be used to help define an effective way to tackle your concerns as well as those of others. We'll be talking more about discipline soon.") Finally, keep the notes for future reference.

Surveys

Surveys can also help identify specific areas where change is needed. They offer the advantage of being able to reach a lot more people in a shorter period of time, and, because they can be confidential and anonymous, respondents are usually more open and frank with their answers and comments. Surveys can range from simple to complex. You will want to develop an approach that suits your school or classroom and community, or you may already have usable data from a current survey.

Included in this chapter are sample opinion surveys specifically worded for major population groups: staff, students, and parents. Assessment tools specifically for the teacher implementing the Positive Discipline program in a single classroom can be found in Chapter 4. The opinion surveys in this chapter are designed to get general information about your school climate, including data about discipline. The one sample survey for staff is focused solely on discipline. At the very least, get this kind of specific input from people on issues they believe should be addressed in your discipline plan. You will need these kinds of data to get students, parents, or a staff to accept any major change in your approach to discipline. Consult a standard reference book if you need help in statistically analyzing any survey you choose to use.

What to Do with Information Gathered

Regardless of what approach you choose, the authors recommend that you do gather data. First of all, gathering data gets others involved in a change process. Second, you will probably gather information that will help you know how to adjust the program to suit your individual needs. Finally, data gathering increases the probability of successful implementation. For example, you may gather indications of staff or parent resistance to change, which will help you know to proceed with care. Or you may gather information that tells you you don't know as much about student attitudes as you thought you knew. As you proceed, you will be prepared.

Self-Assessment

	Yes	No
1. Are my classroom expectations consistent with school rules?	___	___
2. Do I scan all areas of my classroom frequently so I know what is happening in all parts of the room?	___	___
3. Do I teach my students survival skills such as how and when to listen to me, and how to follow directions or ask for help?	___	___
4. Do I provide frequent, specific, positive feedback on both academic work and behavior?	___	___
5. Are personal and social skills taught through lessons on conversing, listening, helping, and sharing?	___	___
6. Are my lessons and materials prepared in advance and taught using a brisk and appropriate pace so students stay on task?	___	___
7. Do I avoid periods of delay and confusion by using smooth, brief transitions between lessons and activities?	___	___
8. Do I use problem-solving activities that avoid win-lose conflicts?	___	___
9. Am I consistent in what I say and do?	___	___
10. Do I follow up on agreements?	___	___
11. Do I treat my students with respect and courtesy?	___	___
12. Do I have high expectations for all students?	___	___
13. Do my students understand the consequences of their choices?	___	___
14. Is group closeness promoted by arranging for cooperative activities, by discouraging competitive cliques, and by being careful not to show favoritism?	___	___
15. Am I knowledgeable about the special characteristics of the various cultures?	___	___

Sample Staff Discipline Survey

Please Return by: _____

To: All Staff
From:
Subject: Discipline

The purpose of this survey is to assess how we, as a staff, feel about discipline in our school. Your honest opinions are important. There are no right or wrong answers. The answers you give and the comments you make will be kept completely confidential. Do not sign your name on this survey unless you want to for some reason.

Thank you for your time and response.

Mark one response per item.

	Strongly Agree	Agree	Disagree	Strongly Disagree
1. I think discipline at our school is great.	A	B	C	D
2. I spend too much time on our present school discipline plan.	A	B	C	D
3. I believe in an all-school discipline plan.	A	B	C	D
4. I think our expectations for our students should be higher.	A	B	C	D
5. I think teachers need support with discipline.	A	B	C	D
6. I think the principal should be involved in the school discipline plan.	A	B	C	D

(continued)

Sample Staff Discipline Survey (continued)

	Strongly Agree	Agree	Disagree	Strongly Disagree
7. I think students should be recognized for appropriate behavior.	A	B	C	D
8. I think the behavior of the few students with problems should not penalize the rest.	A	B	C	D
9. I think parents need to be supportive of school discipline.	A	B	C	D
10. I think developing self-discipline in students is important.	A	B	C	D

Comments: _____

_____

_____

_____

Sample Staff Opinion Survey

Please Return by: _____

To: All Staff
From:
Subject: Staff Opinion Survey

The purpose of this survey is to help us determine how we feel about our school and its related services. Your honest opinions are important. There are no right or wrong answers. The answers you give will be completely confidential. Do not sign your name on this survey unless you want to for some reason.

Thank you for your time and response.

Mark one response per item.

	Strongly Agree	Agree	Disagree	Strongly Disagree
Climate				
1. I think the people at this school care about me as a person.	A	B	C	D
2. I am proud to be a part of this school.	A	B	C	D
3. The building is attractive, pleasant, and clean.	A	B	C	D
4. The overall discipline of students is generally satisfactory.	A	B	C	D
5. When I have a school problem, the staff tries hard to help me solve my problem.	A	B	C	D
6. This school is an orderly and safe place for students to learn.	A	B	C	D

(continued)

Sample Staff Opinion Survey *(continued)*

	Strongly Agree	Agree	Disagree	Strongly Disagree
7. Students are happy at school	A	B	C	D

Achievement

8. The staff finds out the learning needs of each student and then helps him or her.	A	B	C	D
9. Reports to parents concerning students' progress are adequate.	A	B	C	D
10. The staff expects each student to do the very best he or she can.	A	B	C	D

Basic Skills

11. In general, we are doing a good job of teaching the basic skills (math, reading, etc.).	A	B	C	D
12. Students have time to practice and maintain basic skills.	A	B	C	D
13. The school offers a good variety of activities (assemblies, special days and weeks) without taking too much time from the basic curriculum.	A	B	C	D

(continued)

Sample Staff Opinion Survey (continued)

	Strongly Agree	Agree	Disagree	Strongly Disagree
Instructional Excellence				
14. The staff tells students when they are doing a good job.	A	B	C	D
15. The teachers know both what to teach and how to teach.	A	B	C	D
16. People tell me when I am doing a good job.	A	B	C	D
Curriculum Content				
17. The things that students should learn are being taught.	A	B	C	D
18. The school helps parents know about what is being taught.	A	B	C	D
Leadership				
19. The principal is involved with what the students are learning.	A	B	C	D
20. The school has goals or plans to improve and I know about them.	A	B	C	D
21. The principal really cares about students.	A	B	C	D

(continued)

Sample Staff Opinion Survey (continued)

	Strongly Agree	Agree	Disagree	Strongly Disagree
22. While I know I can't have a vote on every decision in this school, I do feel that I can have some say about some decisions.	A	B	C	D

Parent Involvement

	Strongly Agree	Agree	Disagree	Strongly Disagree
23. The staff encourages parents to be involved at school.	A	B	C	D
24. It is easy to make appointments to talk to the staff at our school.	A	B	C	D

Comments: _____
_____
_____
_____

Sample Student Opinion Survey

Please Return by: _____

To: All Students
From:
Subject: Student Opinion Survey

The purpose of this survey is to help us know how you feel about your school. There are no right or wrong answers. Be very honest. Your answers will be kept secret. Do not put your name on your survey unless you want to for some reason. Each question will be read aloud by your teacher. If you don't understand the question, raise your hand and ask about it. Circle your answer in the appropriate column.

Mark only one letter per question.

	Strongly Agree	Agree	Disagree	Strongly Disagree
Climate				
1. I think the students, teachers, and staff at my school care about me.	A	B	C	D
2. I am proud to be a part of this school.	A	B	C	D
3. This school is attractive, pleasant, and clean.	A	B	C	D
4. The behavior of the students is generally OK.	A	B	C	D
5. When I have a school problem, the teacher tries hard to help me work on it and solve the problem.	A	B	C	D

(continued)

Sample Student Opinion Survey (continued)

	Strongly Agree	Agree	Disagree	Strongly Disagree
6. This school is an orderly and safe place for me to learn.	A	B	C	D
7. I am happy at this school.	A	B	C	D

Achievement

	Strongly Agree	Agree	Disagree	Strongly Disagree
8. My teachers find out what I need to learn and then help me learn.	A	B	C	D
9. Reports to my parents about my school work are sent often enough and tell them what they need to know.	A	B	C	D
10. My teachers expect me to do the very best I can.	A	B	C	D
11. My teachers are doing a good job of teaching the basic skills (math, reading, and so forth).	A	B	C	D
12. I have time to practice and use the basic skills I have learned.	A	B	C	D

(continued)

Sample Student Opinion Survey (continued)

	Strongly Agree	Agree	Disagree	Strongly Disagree
13. We have a good variety of special activities (assemblies, special days and weeks) without taking too much time from our learning.	A	B	C	D

Instructional Excellence

14. My teachers tell me when I am doing a good job.	A	B	C	D
15. My teachers know both what to teach and how to teach.	A	B	C	D
16. I tell my teachers when they are doing a good job.	A	B	C	D

Curriculum Content

17. The things that I am learning are the things I should be taught.	A	B	C	D
18. The school helps my parents know about what I am learning.	A	B	C	D

Leadership

19. The principal knows about what I am learning.	A	B	C	D

(continued)

Sample Student Opinion Survey (continued)

	Strongly Agree	Agree	Disagree	Strongly Disagree
20. The school has goals or plans to improve and I know about them.	A	B	C	D
21. The principal really cares about students.	A	B	C	D
22. While I know I can't have a vote on every decision in this school, I do feel that I can have some say about some decisions.	A	B	C	D

Parent Involvement

	Strongly Agree	Agree	Disagree	Strongly Disagree
23. My parents are asked to be involved at school.	A	B	C	D
24. It is easy for parents to make appointments to talk to teachers and school staff.	A	B	C	D

Comments: _____
_____
_____
_____

Sample Parent Opinion Survey

Please Return by: _____

To: Parents and Guardians
From:
Subject: Parent Opinion Survey

The purpose of this survey is to assist the school staff in determining how parents feel about the school and its related services. Your honest opinions are important. There are no right or wrong answers. The answers you give will be completely confidential. Do not sign your name on this survey unless you want to for some reason.

If you have more than one child attending our school, please answer each question as it applies to the oldest child and return only one survey form.

Directions for Returning the Survey

1. Please answer all questions in an honest manner. Choose only one answer, circling the letter under the most appropriate response.
2. Place the completed survey in the attached envelope and seal it.
3. Have your child bring it to school and drop it in the box by the front door.

Mark only one response per question:

	Strongly Agree	Agree	Disagree	Strongly Disagree
Climate				
1. The school staff cares about me and my child.	A	B	C	D
2. My family is proud to be a part of this school.	A	B	C	D
3. The school is attractive, clean, and pleasant.	A	B	C	D
4. The overall discipline of students is generally satisfactory.	A	B	C	D

(continued)

Sample Parent Opinion Survey (continued)

	Strongly Agree	Agree	Disagree	Strongly Disagree
5. When my family has a school problem, the staff tries hard to help us solve it.	A	B	C	D
6. This school is an orderly and safe place for my child to learn.	A	B	C	D
7. My child is happy at this school.	A	B	C	D

Achievement

	Strongly Agree	Agree	Disagree	Strongly Disagree
8. The staff finds out the learning needs of my child and then helps him or her.	A	B	C	D
9. Reports from school concerning my child's progress are adequate.	A	B	C	D
10. The staff expects my child to do the very best he or she can.	A	B	C	D

Basic Skills

	Strongly Agree	Agree	Disagree	Strongly Disagree
11. In general, the teachers are doing a good job of teaching my child the basic skills (math, reading, etc.).	A	B	C	D

(continued)

Sample Parent Opinion Survey (continued)

	Strongly Agree	Agree	Disagree	Strongly Disagree
12. Students have time to practice and maintain basic skills.	A	B	C	D
13. A good variety of activities are provided (assemblies, special days and weeks, etc.) without taking too much time from the basic curriculum areas.	A	B	C	D

Instructional Excellence

	Strongly Agree	Agree	Disagree	Strongly Disagree
14. The staff tells students when they are doing a good job.	A	B	C	D
15. My child's teachers know both what to teach and how to teach.	A	B	C	D
16. My family tells teachers when they are doing a good job.	A	B	C	D

Curriculum Content

	Strongly Agree	Agree	Disagree	Strongly Disagree
17. The things that my child should be learning are being taught.	A	B	C	D

(*continued*)

Sample Parent Opinion Survey (continued)

	Strongly Agree	Agree	Disagree	Strongly Disagree
18. The school helps parents know about what is being taught.	A	B	C	D

Leadership

19. The principal is involved with what my child is learning.	A	B	C	D
20. The school has goals or plans to improve and I know about them.	A	B	C	D
21. The principal really cares about students.	A	B	C	D
22. While I know I can't have a vote on every decision in this school, I do feel that I can have some say about some decisions.	A	B	C	D

Parent Involvement

23. I feel I am encouraged to be involved at school.	A	B	C	D
24. It is easy to make appointments with or talk to the staff.	A	B	C	D

Comments: _____

_____

_____

SECTION II

CLASSROOM DESIGN

CHAPTER 4

Planning for Classroom Implementation

Introduction

Positive Discipline can be implemented in a single classroom as well as throughout an entire school. As a teacher, one of the authors used Positive Discipline, in its unwritten form, while the school in general made no changes. Year after year, the author's principal would say, "You always take the students I give you and they learn to manage their behavior." A district art instructor told the same author, "I love to teach your kids. They are so open and responsive. Do you drown the rebels?" Looking back now, the author believes the principles of Positive Discipline were effectively at work.

Another of the authors, a practicing classroom teacher, moved this year from her original Positive Discipline school. She is implementing the parts of Positive Discipline that fit with her new school and classroom situation. Although her new school has not implemented Positive Discipline school wide, much of the basic philosophy and many of the terms and techniques are in place.

If you want to implement Positive Discipline in your classroom, Chapters 4 and 5 as well as the appendix will be the chapters most useful to you. The authors recommend you review or skim Chapters 1 and 2, then read Chapters 4 and 5 with care. It is important that you understand the Positive Discipline approach and each step of the process before trying to proceed with implementation in your classroom. Practical suggestions for each step are provided. You will also want to skim the appendix.

Teachers spend a great deal of time planning and implementing their particular philosophy of discipline. Sometimes our methods are effective, but more often, we teachers are not pleased with the discipline plan we are using primarily because most discipline plans put the teacher in the role of enforcer of the rules. Students often feel that "anything goes if you don't get caught." We believe the Positive Discipline program can change this scenario by helping students become responsible for making wise decisions. Thus the role of the teacher becomes one of helping children learn to choose wisely.

The Positive Discipline program is a system for teaching appropriate behaviors and wise decision making reinforced by a system of positive recognition and privileges. The responsibility for discipline is shared by the teacher with the students. When a student in your classroom has a behavior problem, your role is one of understanding and support because the student is the one held responsible for his or her behavior and decision making.

Although all rights are reserved, the Reproduction Pages throughout this book may be reproduced or revised for use with this text, provided such reproductions bear the copyright notice. Use this program guide as a handy reference whenever you need to refresh or refocus your efforts.

THE POSITIVE DISCIPLINE PHILOSOPHY

Virtually all students can and will master the skills needed to function appropriately in the school community if given adequate instruction, sufficient time, and support.

Positive Discipline is based on the belief that students can be taught to make appropriate decisions about their own well-being and the well-being of others almost all the time. Even if you have already done so, once again please read page 5 in Chapter 1. Only when you can accept this simple but powerful philosophy will you be able to implement this program successfully.

Step-by-Step to Positive Discipline

The easiest way to understand the Positive Discipline approach in a single classroom is to visualize it as a step-by-step process with several avenues toward success or "feedback loops." Figure 4–1, shown on page 97, illustrates the relationship between each step.

Understanding Each Step of the Positive Discipline Flowchart

The flowchart is very much like the flowchart discussed in Chapter 2. Only a few adjustments have been made to adapt the flowchart to the single classroom.

Assessment

You wouldn't be reading this book if you were completely satisfied with the discipline in your classroom. Think about why you believe you may be ready for a change. Review the materials in Chapter 3. The Sample Student Opinion Survey and the Sample Parent Opinion Survey included in Chapter 3 have been revised for use in a single classroom and are included at the end of this chapter. Select the methods which appeal to you or design your own assessment. Don't be tempted to skip the assessment step. At the minimum, put a few thoughts on paper as well as a few, brief, daily notes concerning current student behaviors. Keep these notes with your Positive Discipline materials for future reference or for when parents, your principal, or a colleague questions you about your program.

Involve Others

Before you go any further in developing your Positive Discipline plan, you will need to visit with your principal. Be prepared to explain why you want to change your discipline plan. Share your self-assessment and suggest ways the principal can be supportive. Parents and guardians also need to be kept aware of your expectations for discipline and how students will be expected to fulfill those expectations. Send home information but make sure the principal has a copy before it is sent home with students. Your students will be going to other classes for instruction (music class, for example). Let the staff know you are teaching, practicing, testing, and reteaching self-discipline. Other teachers will be cooperative in working with discipline concerns if they are well informed of your discipline plan. You will also need to recruit those people who could become part of your Support Group. Be sure they will have time available to become involved.

Determine Classroom Expectations

Expectations are replacements for *the rules*. Rules are imposed by someone in a superior position. Expectations are developed cooperatively by people working together to create an environment were everyone can succeed and feel they belong. Expectations provide guidelines for personal behavior and decision making. Key Concept 1, "Determining Expectations," (see Chapter 2) contains specific details for your consideration. Share the four decision-making areas with the students: achievement, interactions, safety, and surroundings. Teach students the difference between rules and expectations. Then involve students in developing expectations for their classroom.

Discipline is more effective when stated in terms of expectations rather than rules. Rules have to be constantly monitored and enforced by the teacher, whereas expectations are monitored by students practicing wise decision making. State expectations simply and define them clearly. Students need to know what the expectations are and why they are needed. It is important to keep classroom expectations to a reasonable number. Students can usually remember and manage three to five classroom expectations.

Teach Expectations and Wise Decision Making

Once classroom expectations are clearly and positively stated in behavioral terms (seeable, countable, and measurable), the next task is to teach these expectations and wise decision making with the same care and clarity used to teach content-area lessons. Students are not expected to know words or numbers when they first come to school. Do not expect them to know how to behave in classroom situations, especially in the large group.

The process is teach, practice, reteach, practice. The teacher "grades" progress on expectations, either verbally or in writing, telling the students what they are doing right. Progress checks and feedback continue throughout the year. There should be intense concentrated practice when establishing the classroom expectations and periodic reteaching once things are going well.

Establish Esprit de Corps

Some of the skills of self-discipline are social. Teach these skills by establishing a warm and caring classroom environment. Teach students how to contribute to that environment by caring for and including each other in activities. Esprit de corps helps students feel good about themselves and able to work toward important group goals. Promote group identity by arranging for cooperative experiences and by discouraging cliques. Only when we feel accepted, cared for, and secure can we contribute and work effectively.

Guided Practice of Expected Behaviors

As wise decision making and expected behaviors are learned, you carefully guide students' practice attempts by providing the same kind of consistent, positive feedback you give for learning reading and math skills. This book presents techniques that encourage you to focus on consistently recognizing successful attempts at wise decision making rather than punishing students' attempts to learn the skills and actions of responsibility and self-discipline. Punishment only stops behavior, it does nothing to build desired behavior. Logical rather than punitive consequences for inappropriate behavior are encouraged. Logical consequences follow as the natural result of behaviors that are not in the students' best interests. Students are involved in problem-solving activities that avoid conflicts. In this way the classroom setting becomes more like the settings students will deal with as adults. Students learn skills and behaviors that will help them cope and survive as effective and responsible adults because they are encouraged to do so in a variety of ways. Extrinsic rewards (external and tangible) are used sparingly. Intrinsic rewards (inner and natural) become the major motivators.

Independent Practice of Expected Behaviors

Guidance is gradually withdrawn as students' skills at being self-disciplined grow. This independent practice period helps to build students' confidence in newly learned skills and allows them to feel the pleasures and joys that come with being successfully self-disciplined.

Diagnostic Progress Check

Since students are human and therefore far from perfect, you continue to provide at least a minimal amount of support as you informally diagnose which students are truly demonstrating consistent self-discipline, which students need more time and support, and which few are going to need more time and support than you alone can provide. Students are encouraged to assess and analyze their own behavior in order to develop critical thinking skills and intrinsic motivation.

Successful Achievers

Successful achievers are encouraged to continue to be self-disciplined and responsible with a weekly special activity time called Classroom Team Time and by becoming members of the classroom team. Members are given special privileges and wear some type of special membership symbol. Almost all people enjoy earning membership in special groups, and children are no exception. The Positive Discipline Classroom Team is unusually special because all students are expected to become members during the school year. The Classroom Team is a nonexclusive group. You and your students all help everyone achieve membership.

Students Needing More Practice

Nonachieving students are divided into two subgroups: "almost achievers" and "problem students." The majority of these nonachievers need only more time and support from you and your classroom group to achieve success. You and the successful achievers work together to provide that support.

Almost Achievers. Almost Achievers receive some additional instruction, more guided practice, and support from you and their classmates who are members of the team. Then, further independent practice takes place followed by a second diagnostic progress check. Almost Achievers will usually move into the ranks of Successful Achievers, and are recognized and awarded privileges.

Problem Students. Sometimes a few students will need more than just additional time and support from you and the classroom group. In these cases, the Positive Discipline Support Group is used to augment the classroom group. Other adults and occasionally a special student friend are identified to provide still more encouragement. Specific behaviors of a student are identified and worked on one at a time. By focusing efforts on one behavior at a time, a nonachieving student has a real chance at being at least partially successful with that one behavior. Guided practice focused on the one identified behavior is given and partial successes are encouraged and rewarded. Independent practice is then again attempted. Success with a single behavior is achieved when that behavior ceases to cause problems for the student. Success breeds further success. Another problem behavior is identified and the cycle continues until this student also becomes self-disciplined and a responsible achiever.

Positive Discipline focuses on stimulating appropriate socialization and on preventing problems. Instruction followed by acknowledging appropriate behavior with a variety of recognition and privileges, is used as the formula for success. Throughout, students are seen as willing, potentially capable and cooperative, but needing guidance, instruction, support, and time for practice in becoming successful decison makers.

Using the Key Concepts in the Classroom

Now that you have reviewed the basics of Positive Discipline, this section reviews the key concepts described in detail in Chapter 2. Practical suggestions to help implement the steps in the flowchart are included.

The authors encourage you to experiment with the materials in the appendix. You may wish to use all of the program materials. If you have developed techniques that work, intersperse them with these procedures. Add and delete to build a strong individualized discipline program for your classroom. An experienced teacher will need only to skim the suggestions and materials. A beginning teacher will want to study some materials and suggestions carefully and perhaps even imagine some realistic situations.

Key Concept 1
Determining Classroom Expectations

Making appropriate decisions in four decision-making areas—achievement, interactions, safety, and surroundings—is really what a happy, productive life is all about. Expectations differ from one classroom to another. Each teacher is aware of how classroom discipline works best for his or her group of students. It is highly recommended that you and your students decide together what the expectations should be for your classroom. Students are willing to fulfill expectations they feel are necessary—ones they understand, and ones they have helped select.

Students are expected to know and follow building rules and, for some, bus rules. They are also required to follow rules established by other teachers (library, music, etc.). Therefore, the fewer expectations selected for the classroom, the easier it becomes for students to be successful. As few as three expectations and as many as five are suggested for you and students to develop. Classroom expectations need to be stated positively so students will know what they are expected to do instead of just what not to do. They also need to be stated behaviorally so all can see when students are behaving as expected. All expectations fit in one of four areas: achievement, interactions, safety, and surroundings. Discuss these areas and have students help select expectations that are in their own individual and in the group's best interest. Some typical classroom expectations are listed below as reference material for use prior to involving students in designing expectations for your classroom.

Sample Classroom Expectations
(Decide on no more than five total.)

Achievement
- Work hard.
- Stay on task.
- Complete assignments.
- Turn in homework.
- Have paper and pencil available.
- Work independently from 9:30–10:00.
- Raise hand if help is needed.
- Put assignments in labeled baskets.

(*continued*)

Key Concept 1 (*continued*)

Interactions
> Be kind.
> Respect each other.
> Treat others as you would like to be treated.
> Leave "personal space" (a comfortable distance between you and the next person).
> Take turns.
> Be recognized before talking.
> One person at a time at the pencil sharpener.

Safety
> Use a pass to leave the room.
> Sign out if leaving the room.
> Keep hands, feet, and objects to self.
> Use equipment safely.

Surroundings
> Respect property.
> Keep desk and floor clean.
> Use indoor voice.
> Gum and candy only with teacher permission.
> Ask permission to take balls outside.
> Clean up after yourself.

Involving Students

One way to involve students in selecting the expectations for a classroom is to set aside about thirty minutes for a classroom meeting. During the meeting, you can discuss the terms *rules* and *expectations*. The point should be made that only students can control their own behavior. You do not have to be an enforcer of rules but can instead act as one whose role is to help students learn, practice, and follow expectations as they achieve self-discipline. The class, including the teacher, can then suggest expectations for the classroom that will help learning take place and help everyone feel a part of the classroom. The classroom group can use either a vote or a consensus procedure to select the three to five expectations for the classroom.

Key Concept 2
The Teaching Model

The authors encourage you to teach expectations with the same care and clarity you teach reading and math. Briefly review the Teaching Model described in Chapter 2. The sample lesson plans in this book are built on the model. If you don't have a standard lesson plan or teaching model, you may wish to try the model with other subjects besides discipline. If you have never used a similar model, begin its use with a lesson to prepare students for the first fire drill of the year.

Key Concept 3
Esprit de Corps

Developing esprit de corps or a highly supportive group spirit is an essential component of the Positive Discipline program. Even experienced teachers will want to review the description of esprit de corps in Chapter 2 as well as the sample lesson plans in the appendix. The lesson plans are adaptable to any grade level. If you feel unsure, consult a trusted peer.

To identify members of a caring classroom, one author takes snapshots of students in groups of three and displays the photos on an award chart. Once a week, two or three students are selected to be featured as caring, helpful, kind friends. The chart also features sentences with the words *caring, helpful,* and *kind.* The award is displayed for a week and then sent home with one of the students on Friday.

During the first three weeks of school, one of the authors watches for opportune moments during the school day to call attention to some caring action shown by a student toward another. It doesn't take any longer to look for and compliment positive actions than it does to point out negative actions. Unless an incident is repeated many times or could cause harm, the author chooses not to comment or show facial disapproval. This approach takes practice on the part of the teacher but it does promote a positive environment.

Sometimes it is possible to point out positive attributes of a class to an adult who steps in the room with a message or comes to pick up a student. Catch the unplanned moment and capitalize on developing a warm and caring classroom students enjoy being part of every day. Most building principals are willing to have students sent to the office for the specific purpose of telling the principal about positive esprit de corps activities.

One afternoon a teacher chose a book to read aloud to the class. The story highlighted an incident between two students that caused one student to have hurt feelings. After the story the teacher guided a discussion of the book and the students contrasted their experience with the incident in the story. The combination classroom of first and second graders prided themselves on talking about feelings, caring, and esprit de corps. The teacher acknowledged their transfer of learning from a Positive Discipline lesson to the story read that day. Of course, the teacher had carefully planned for the reinforcement lesson on esprit de corps to take place that afternoon.

(continued)

Key Concept 3 (*continued*)

Encourage family members to ask the child about caring activities at school. At Open House or during individual parent conferences, encourage parents to ask their child, "What caring thing happened at school today?" This involvement of parents causes students to become very aware of their actions and the actions of their peers.

Key Concept 4
What to Do When Students Choose Wisely

In order to teach students self-discipline, you will need to make a concerted effort to recognize and positively reinforce students' appropriate behavior as you teach expected behaviors. Review Key Concept 4 in Chapter 2. List additional recognition activities for use in your classroom.

Key Concept 5
The Classroom Team

Refer to Key Concept 5 in Chapter 2 and select some of the ideas concerning a team. You will want to let students know a team will be formed. Don't be concerned about all students desiring team membership. In the authors' experience, even the most resistant boys and girls work hard to earn team membership, especially when they are given appropriate support and encouragement.

Key Concept 6
What to Do When Students Choose Unwisely

Using positive recognition and reinforcement for appropriate behavior is critical to the success of the program, but knowing effective techniques to use with inappropriate behavior is also necessary. A quick review of the material in Key Concept 6 in Chapter 2 will help refresh your memory or add to your "bag of tricks."

Positive Discipline stresses the use of logical rather than punitive consequences for inappropriate behavior. Logical consequences are directly related to a student's behavior, delivered with a tone of regret, and carefully explained to the student. Think of some personal experiences you've had as you read about logical consequences.

An additional technique for your consideration is the Silent Conference. This technique is one way to address misbehavior in an inconspicuous and relatively nonconfrontive way.

Silent Conferences

The purpose of holding a silent conference is to minimize the amount of teacher time involved and/or potential disruption to the normal flow of learning. It is a good technique to use when feeling levels are high, when students from other rooms are involved, and when time is short and you need to get on with lessons. It can be used for problems such as talking out or an argument between people (student and student or teacher and student.)

The "What Happened?" and the "What Is the Problem?" Silent Conferences

Ask the students who are involved to sit down. Supply them with pencils and papers and have them write down what happened and what they each did. You may also want them to write about what they could have done instead. (The authors suggest you keep a supply of the two forms included here.) Writing both what happened and what they each did will help children vent frustrations and get them to focus on the real problem. It will also save time for the teacher. (One can read a lot faster than listen.) After written information has been obtained, other data can quickly be gathered and a fair decision made. Students will have some very inventive spellings you may need to clarify. If students from other rooms are involved (especially after recess) be sure to let their teacher know their location. It is even possible to give students a "What Hap-

(continued)

What Happened?

What happened?

What did you do?

What could you have done instead?

What Is the Problem?

Name two great things about you.

What is the problem?

What do you need to do to solve the problem?

Will things be better for you when you solve the problem? How?

List the steps you will take to solve the problem.

Who will need to help you with the steps of your plan?

You need to keep track of your progress and reward yourself for progress everyday. How will you do that?

What do you think the results of your plan will be?

Key Concept 6 (*continued*)

pened?" or a "What Is the Problem?" form and let them complete it in their own rooms.

The "Problem Solving" Silent Conference

Let's say you are having a problem with a student interrupting and talking without permission. Normally, this student isn't a big problem, but today he is really getting to you. Grab a sheet of paper or a large filing card and start a silent conference. You can go right on with activities. On the paper or file card, explain your perception of the problem. For example, write:

> "John, today you are having trouble raising your hand before you talk. You do not usually have this trouble. What is the problem?"

Now, hand the paper to John. Encourage him, nonverbally, to write his answer on the paper. He might write:

> "I don't know."

You then take the paper back and write:

> "Can you get this under control?"

Again, hand the paper to John. He might write:

> "Yes."

You then write:

> "Good!"

Of course, this is a very simple example, but it should give you the general idea. Some teachers like to use a standard 4" x 5" card for silent conferences. They can be dated and kept in a card file for future reference.

Finally, another technique recommended by the authors to deal with inappropriate behavior is a Problem-Solving Session. You may have used a similar technique. If so, use your own meth-

(*continued*)

Key Concept 6 (*continued*)

ods. Additional ideas about problem solving sessions can be found on pages 000–000 in the appendix.

Problem-Solving Sessions

Although lessons on common school problem areas (Conflict Resolution, Manage Your Fate, and Go with the Flow) are included in the appendix, no one can anticipate every problem any one class may have. Each class has a personality and accompanying problems of its own. Some groups are prone to lying, putting each other down, or rumor passing; others are not. Frequently it doesn't do much good to tell the class to stop. The authors have found class problem-solving sessions to be helpful whenever a unique problem arises.

A classroom problem-solving session involves setting aside twenty to thirty minutes of class time to discuss the problem, brainstorm solutions, and devise a system of evaluating progress toward correcting the problem. Begin by writing a clear statement of the problem on the board.

The following sample problem-solving outline will give you a good idea of how to get started on a problem-solving session:

Problem: _____

What's happening now?

What should be happening?

What needs to be done?

Who is going to do it?

Time line?

How will we know we're finished?

Next, have the students assist with answering the questions about an identified problem similar to the example below.

Problem: Name calling is causing a lot of our classmates to feel unhappy.

(continued)

Key Concept 6 (*continued*)

What's happening now?

There's too much name calling.

What should be happening?

Everyone should be saying only nice things about each other.

What needs to be done?

We need to say nothing at all if we can't say something nice.

Who is going to do it?

We are!

Time line?

One week.

How will we know we're finished?

No reports of name calling for one week.

Key Concept 7
Students Needing More Practice

Almost Achievers

One key to helping those students who do not at first demonstrate appropriate decision making is to involve them in analyzing their own decisions. Also, the more positive encouragement and recognition you can provide, the more quickly these students will achieve success.

Problem Students

You will need to recruit and train people for your Support Group. Reread the material in Chapter 2 about the Support Group. As you read, potential Support Group members will come to mind.

You will also find that devising an Intervention Contract will help with those students who are making little or no progress. First, do some serious thinking about one student's behaviors. Make a list of the behaviors you would like to see the student change. State these behaviors positively so the student will know what to do instead of what not to do. Next, select just the ones that are seriously interfering with this student's learning. Now eliminate any that (1) cannot be taught and monitored consistently, (2) are not reasonable expectations for this student's grade level, (3) cannot be stated positively, and (4) cannot be seen and counted on a daily basis. Pick just one or two to discuss with the student.

Next, with the student, devise a contract. Target one behavior at a time. Include a method for keeping track of and recognizing progress. Then help the student select the Support Group members. Persons selected should be "significant others" to the student and may include such people as the physical education or music teacher, the principal, a former teacher, a counselor, a parent, and occasionally a peer or another student. Tell the student the persons selected will be aware of the contract and will keep in contact with the student about progress.

Ask the Support Group members to make a special effort to contact the student frequently about progress. Contacts need not be time-consuming—just a brief, positive word or two in passing is all that is needed. Recycle the system until the student is ready for the next step. Then target another single behavior. You may find, as the authors did, while the student is working on the first targeted behavior, one or two other behaviors are corrected. Sometimes, only one contract need be devised. When the student sat-

(continued)

Key Concept 7 (*continued*)

isfactorily completes the necessary cycles of the contract, he or she enters the Achiever category and becomes eligible for the classroom club.

Note: Occasionally a student may not respond to the caring that can be established by the Support Group and may need to be referred to the special education process. However, it is very important not to give up too quickly. A good rule of thumb is to work with the student for at least ten weeks before deciding absolutely no progress has been made. Virtually all children will make some progress toward appropriate behavior when given enough support.

If you become discouraged about a particular student, reread the section in Chapter 2 entitled More Information about Problem Students and/or refer to materials in the appendix.

Student Intervention Contract

Student's Name _____ Teacher _____ Room____

Student's Strengths _____

_____

_____

Team Members (3–5) _____ _____

_____ _____

_____

Target behavior:

Student's statement about what is to be done about the target behavior:

Recognition/Privileges to be provided for achievement:

_____

_____

_____

_____

Student Signature

(Please see reverse side)

Teacher's Notes:

A. GUIDED PRACTICE

Who guides practice? _____

Checkpoint date(s): _____

B. INDEPENDENT PRACTICE

Checkpoint date _____

Teacher's evaluation of success _____

_____

_____

            _____   _____

               Date   Teacher Signature

Figure 4–1. Classroom Flowchart

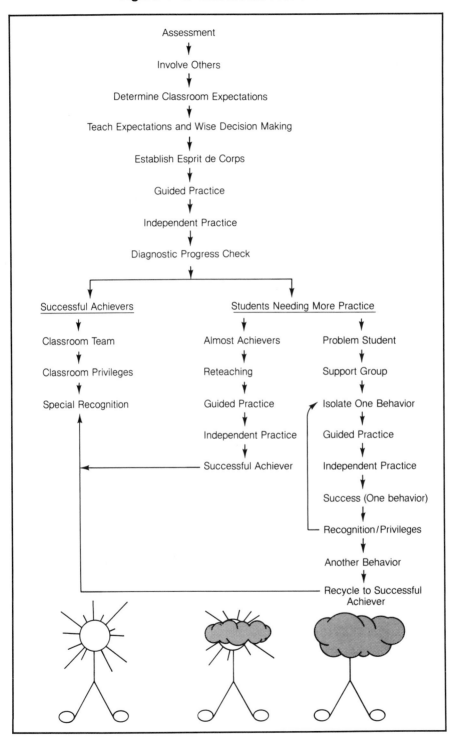

Assessment
↓
Involve Others
↓
Determine Classroom Expectations
↓
Teach Expectations and Wise Decision Making
↓
Establish Esprit de Corps
↓
Guided Practice
↓
Independent Practice
↓
Diagnostic Progress Check

Successful Achievers
↓
Classroom Team
↓
Classroom Privileges
↓
Special Recognition

Students Needing More Practice

Almost Achievers
↓
Reteaching
↓
Guided Practice
↓
Independent Practice
↓
Successful Achiever

Problem Student
↓
Support Group
↓
Isolate One Behavior
↓
Guided Practice
↓
Independent Practice
↓
Success (One behavior)
↓
Recognition / Privileges
↓
Another Behavior
↓
Recycle to Successful Achiever

Sample Student Opinion Survey for an Individual Classroom

Please Return by: _____

To: All Classroom Students
From:
Subject: Student Opinion Survey

    The purpose of this survey is to help us know how you feel about your classroom. There are no right or wrong answers. Be very honest. Your answers will be kept secret. Do not put your name on your survey unless you want to for some reason. Each question will be read aloud by your teacher. If you don't understand the question, raise your hand and ask about it. Circle your answer in the appropriate column.

Mark only one letter per question.

Climate	Strongly Agree	Agree	Disagree	Strongly Disagree
1. I think the teacher and the students in my classroom care about me.	A	B	C	D
2. I am proud to be a part of this class.	A	B	C	D
3. This classroom is attractive, pleasant, and clean.	A	B	C	D
4. The behavior of the students is generally O.K.	A	B	C	D
5. When I have a school problem, the teacher tries hard to help me work on it and solve the problem.	A	B	C	D
6. This classroom is an orderly and safe place for me to learn.	A	B	C	D
7. I am happy in this classroom.	A	B	C	D

(*continued*)

Sample Student Opinion Survey for an Individual Classroom
(continued)

	Strongly Agree	Agree	Disagree	Strongly Disagree
Achievement				
8. My teacher finds out what I need to learn and then helps me learn it.	A	B	C	D
9. Reports to my parents about my school work are sent often enough and tell them what they need to know.	A	B	C	D
10. My teacher expects me to do the very best I can.	A	B	C	D
11. My teacher is doing a good job of teaching the basic skills (math, reading, and so forth).	A	B	C	D
12. I have time to practice and use the basic skills I have learned.	A	B	C	D
13. We have a good variety of special activities (special events, special days and weeks) without taking too much time from our learning.	A	B	C	D

(continued)

Sample Student Opinion Survey for an Individual Classroom
(continued)

	Strongly Agree	Agree	Disagree	Strongly Disagree
Instructional Excellence				
14. My teacher tells me when I am doing a good job.	A	B	C	D
15. My teacher knows both what to teach and how to teach.	A	B	C	D
16. I tell my teacher when he or she is doing a good job.	A	B	C	D
Curriculum Content				
17. The things that I am learning are the things I should be taught.	A	B	C	D
18. The teacher helps my parents know about what I am learning.	A	B	C	D
Leadership				
19. The classroom has goals or plans to improve and I know about them.	A	B	C	D
20. The teacher really cares about the students.	A	B	C	D

(continued)

Sample Student Opinion Survey for an Individual Classroom
(continued)

	Strongly Agree	Agree	Disagree	Strongly Disagree
21. While I know I can't have a vote on every decision in this classroom, I do feel that I can have some say about some decisions.	A	B	C	D

Parent Involvement

	Strongly Agree	Agree	Disagree	Strongly Disagree
22. My parents are asked to be involved in this classroom.	A	B	C	D
23. It is easy for parents to make appointments to talk to my teacher.	A	B	C	D

Comments: _____

_____

_____

_____

Sample Parent Opinion Survey
for Use in an Individual Classroom

Please Return by: _____

To: Parents and Guardians

From:

Subject: Parent Opinion Survey

The purpose of this survey is to assist me in determining how parents feel about my classroom. Your honest opinions are important. There are no right or wrong answers. The answers you give will be completely confidential. Do not sign your name on this survey unless you want to for some reason.

Directions for Returning the Survey

1. Please answer all questions in an honest manner. Choose only one answer, circling the letter under the most appropriate response.
2. Place the completed survey in the attached envelope and seal it.
3. Have your child bring it to school and drop it in the box by the classroom door.

Mark only one response per question.

Climate	Strongly Agree	Agree	Disagree	Strongly Disagree
1. I think the teacher cares about me and my child.	A	B	C	D
2. My child is proud to be a part of this classroom.	A	B	C	D
3. The classroom is attractive, pleasant, and clean.	A	B	C	D
4. The overall discipline of students is generally satisfactory.	A	B	C	D

(continued)

Sample Parent Opinion Survey (continued)

	Strongly Agree	Agree	Disagree	Strongly Disagree
5. When my child has a school problem, the teacher tries hard to help us work on and solve it.	A	B	C	D
6. This classroom is an orderly and safe place for my child to learn.	A	B	C	D
7. My child is happy in this classroom.	A	B	C	D

Achievement

	Strongly Agree	Agree	Disagree	Strongly Disagree
8. The teacher finds out the learning needs of my child and then helps him or her.	A	B	C	D
9. Reports from the classroom concerning my child's progress are adequate.	A	B	C	D
10. The teacher expects my child to do the very best he or she can.	A	B	C	D

Basic Skills

	Strongly Agree	Agree	Disagree	Strongly Disagree
11. In general, the teacher is doing a good job of teaching my child the basic skills (math, reading, etc.).	A	B	C	D

(continued)

Sample Parent Opinion Survey (continued)

	Strongly Agree	Agree	Disagree	Strongly Disagree
12. My child has time to practice and maintain basic skills.	A	B	C	D
13. A good variety of activities are provided (special events, special days and weeks, etc.) without taking too much time from the basic curriculum areas.	A	B	C	D

Instructional Excellence

	Strongly Agree	Agree	Disagree	Strongly Disagree
14. The teacher tells my child when he or she is doing a good job.	A	B	C	D
15. My child's teacher knows both what to teach and how to teach.	A	B	C	D
16. My family tells the teacher when he or she is doing a good job.	A	B	C	D

Curriculum Content

	Strongly Agree	Agree	Disagree	Strongly Disagree
17. The things that my child should be learning are being taught.	A	B	C	D
18. The teacher helps me know about what is being taught.	A	B	C	D

(continued)

Sample Parent Opinion Survey (continued)

	Strongly Agree	Agree	Disagree	Strongly Disagree
Leadership				
20. The classroom has goals or plans to improve and I know about them.	A	B	C	D
21. The teacher really cares about students.	A	B	C	D
22. While I know I can't have a vote on every decision for this classroom, I do feel that I can have some say about some decisions.	A	B	C	D
Parent Involvement				
23. I feel I am encouraged to be involved in the classroom.	A	B	C	D
24. It is easy to make appointments with or talk to the teacher.	A	B	C	D

Comments: _____

_____

_____

CHAPTER 5

Implementing Positive Discipline in the Classroom

Now that you have a general view of the program, you are ready to implement it. This chapter contains a suggested time line. The time line will be most helpful if you gather the support materials from the end of this chapter and the appendix and make your own packet for each week containing the activities and the materials suggested. This will help you quickly review concepts when needed and will help you have lesson plans and other materials available as they are needed. Lesson plans and record-keeping charts are located in the appendix and are ordered alphabetically. Materials for parents are located at the end of this chapter and are numbered consecutively. Activities are planned for seven weeks and are divided into weekly segments.

Positive Discipline Time Line: Week 1

The authors of the Positive Discipline program strongly recommend concentrating on teaching behavior during the first three weeks of implementation. This is supported by the research done by Emmer and Evertson (referred to in Chapter 1). Consequently, do not expect to do as much as you usually do with academic subjects. Once Positive Discipline has been established, you can expect to go faster and further with academic subjects. In the long run, you will save both time and effort.

Before beginning, review the flowchart and the Key Concepts in Chapter 2 once more. The suggested lessons and activities for this week as well as the next two are numerous, but we urge you to do them thoroughly. You will find that the time and effort will be well spent. Support materials are found in the appendix and at the end of the chapter. Most of all, have some fun with the suggested lessons and activities this week!

Teacher Activities	Support Materials
• Introduce Positive Discipline.	• Introducing Positive Discipline (A)
• Determine classroom expectations.	
• Teach and practice expectations.	• Go with the Flow (B)
	• Playground Expectations (C)
• Provide consistent recognition for success.	
• Provide logical consequences for inappropriate behavior.	
• Begin to build esprit de corps.	• Esprit de Corps Lessons 1 & 2 (D & E)
• Teach conflict resolution.	• Conflict Resolution (F)
• Teach alternatives to fighting.	• Manage Your Fate (G)
• Experiment with silent conferences.	
• Send introduction letter to parents.	• Parent Letter (letter 1)

Positive Discipline Time Line: Week 2

Hopefully, many students are already exhibiting consistently appropriate behavior and you are enjoying giving praise to those students. If you cannot remember the essential attributes of what to do when students choose wisely or unwisely, reread Key Concepts 4 and 5 in Chapter 2. This week you have several suggested activities to complete and three new lessons to teach. Remember—concentrate on thoroughly teaching behavior now, and you will have easy going later.

Teacher Activities	*Support Materials*
• Review all expectations.	
• Provide guided practice for all expectations.	
• Continue to build esprit de corps.	• Esprit de Corps Lessons 3, 4, 5 (H, I, J)
• Continue to provide recognition for success and logical consequences for inappropriate behavior.	
• Try a silent conference.	
• Discuss the Classroom Team.	

Have a super week!

Positive Discipline Time Line: Week 3

It is very important that you review all the expectations carefully and do a conscientious job of guiding practice this week. Give lots of positive verbal recognition for appropriate behavior. Maybe you could use a spelling bee or other game to review the expectations. Be sure that any new students who join your classroom have direct instruction about the expectations. You may wish to assign buddies or partners who will help new students practice and learn how to behave appropriately. This week be sure to plan a short Team Time activity for all students who are making progress. Try not to leave anyone out of Team Time this week.

Teacher Activities

- Review all expectations.
- Provide abundant guided practice.
- Provide abundant verbal recognition for success.
- Provide group recognition for progress (Team Time).
- Provide logical consequences for inappropriate behavior.
- Continue to build esprit de corps.
- Hold a problem-solving session.
- Finalize details of the Classroom Team and share the plans with the principal.

Support Materials

- Esprit de Corps Lesson 6 (K)

What you expect is what you get!

Positive Discipline Time Line: Week 4

If you have done a thorough job of teaching behavior during the first three weeks, the hard work should begin paying off now. Your academic lessons should go smoothly if you have firmly established the expectations and students are enjoying the benefits of wise decision making.

Positive Discipline "sponges" are included this week. Sponges are short learning activities that can be used to soak up time (like a sponge) during idle moments, including the time when students are waiting for others to get drinks, while the class is waiting for some students to return from a special class, or during the few minutes you might occasionally have when you finish a lesson earlier than planned. Most sponges are short, whole-class activities that do not have to be graded. Sponges can turn lost time into learning time.

For example, after finishing a lesson you have three minutes until time to go to recess. Begin the process of lining up for recess. While students are lining up, have students name some ways they plan to be conscious of safety on the playground. Or you might say, "Thumbs up if you think two people should go down the slide at the same time. Thumbs down if you don't." On mornings when some students haven't yet arrived, use a sponge to review the expectations for assemblies. The sponges suggested (Handout L in the appendix) are all to be done orally. Feel free to develop your own activities that use the blackboard, a worksheet, or an overhead projector.

You will be asking students to do some higher level thinking this week as they analyze and evaluate their own behavior. Analyzing and evaluating are component parts of the decision-making process. Select from among the student record-keeping charts in the appendix or feel free to design your own. Again, provide a short Team Time activity to recognize progress this week.

Teacher Activities	*Support Materials*
• Review expectations and the four areas by using sponges.	• Positive Discipline Sponges (L)
• Provide recognition and logical consequences including Team Time.	• Brain Power (M)
	• Staying on Task (N)
	• Gossip (O)
	• Making Choices (P)
• Continue to build esprit de corps.	• Esprit de Corps Lesson 7 (Q)

(continued)

Positive Discipline Time Line: Week 4 (*continued*)

Teacher Activities

- Introduce independent practice.

- Have students complete at least two self-analysis charts during the week.

- Diagnose students' progress by reviewing the record-keeping charts to see if you agree with the students.

Support Materials

- Introducing Independent Practice (R)
- Self-Analysis Charts: Positive Discipline Skills
  My Choices Today/ This Week

Hard work pays dividends!

Positive Discipline Time Line: Week 5

This week is "catch-up" week or "coast" week, depending on what you have accomplished so far.

Teacher Activities

- Review expectations by using sponges.
- Provide recognition, logical consequences, and Team Time.
- Provide guided practice and correctives.
- Provide independent practice and extensions for students who are ready.
- Have students complete self-analysis charts bi-weekly or weekly.
- Continue to diagnose student progress.

Definition of a genius: A person who aims at something no one else can see and hits it.

Positive Discipline Time Line: Week 6

Your first induction ceremony may be held this week. You will want to reassure those who are not eligible for membership at this time. Tell them you expect them to become members soon and let them tell you what they will do in order to become eligible for membership. You may want to inform the parents of students who are not yet ready for club membership. You can plan another induction ceremony in a week or two. Talk more about esprit de corps with all the students and get everyone helping everyone to become members. A Team Time for all those making progress will help.

Teacher Activities

- Review expectations.
- Continue to provide recognition, logical consequences, guided and independent practice, and correctives/extensions.
- Sign certificates for the induction ceremony.
- Meet with students who need Intervention Contracts.
- Notify parents of Achievers and Almost Achievers.

Support Materials

- Sample Letter: Positive Discipline Achiever (letter 2)
- Sample Letter: Positive Discipline Progress (letter 3)

**School is a magic place
where together we make tomorrow.**

Positive Discipline Time Line: Week 7

You should be experiencing much satisfaction from your efforts. The feeling of satisfaction will increase as you maintain the Positive Discipline program in the coming weeks. The next section contains suggestions for maintaining the program.

Teacher Activities

- Hold induction ceremony.
- Begin Intervention Contracts.

Support Materials

Various support materials can be found at the end of this chapter (sample Parent Letters 1, 2, and 3) as well as in the appendix.

Keeping Positive Discipline Exciting and Motivating in the Classroom

Once Positive Discipline is in place, it will be necessary to monitor, adjust, and evaluate the program. You will need to accommodate changes that occur after you begin the program, especially when new students arrive. The authors have included several topics and tips that worked for us during the first year of implementation in our schools. The process of leading students toward the development of self-discipline is a continuing challenge and a dynamic opportunity to meet the needs of today and tomorrow.

If You Have a Difficult Class

The Positive Discipline program will make a potentially difficult year easier. Nevertheless, the teacher who has a difficult class will be faced with a challenge. The establishment of esprit de corps is especially essential with a difficult class. This sense of "family" creates tremendous peer support for self-discipline. After using the suggested lessons to teach esprit de corps, a difficult class particularly needs class meetings.

Do not hesitate to have a daily class meeting with a group having difficulties. In one classroom, a difficult group of students wrote agenda items in a specified place on the blackboard. When the time arrived for the daily classroom meeting, the discussion began with the first item on the list. Meetings were limited to fifteen minutes each day. The student who placed the item on the agenda "owned" the concern and led the discussion. Classmates were asked for possible solutions. The class worked on the concern until a consensus decision was reached. Sometimes it took three or four meetings to reach an agreeable, reasonable solution for just one agenda item. For other items, only a portion of a meeting was used. The second item on the agenda was not discussed until the first concern was resolved. The teacher wisely refrained from interfering in the group's processing, even though it occasionally felt like the students were just wasting precious instructional time. As the year progressed, group process helped the group develop a stronger feeling of group esprit de corps. As the students helped create solutions, they built their commitment to helping each other solve problems and address concerns.

For example, Debra and Joseph constantly accused each other of forgetting to put the caps back on the magic markers at the drawing center. Other students joined in the conflict and began to take sides in the issue. Soon the problem extended to recess time and other students joined in the conflict. Debra finally put the problem on the class meeting agenda. It took twelve minutes of thinking and suggesting before Joseph's best buddy, Steven, suggested that he could be a friend to both students and double check on the caps before going home each day. The arrangement was agreeable to the class. Shy Steven showed caring and helpfulness and developed into a class leader as the year progressed. That particular class meeting was the beginning of the development of Steven's leadership ability.

In another incident, the class was dissatisfied with the way the teacher had set up the schedule for use of the traveling computer during "free choice time." It took five full class meetings for the group to brainstorm and argue over the computer schedule. Finally, the class agreed to pair "knowledgeable computer whizzes" with less knowledgeable students. At first glance, it would have been easier for the teacher to return the computer to the multi-media room, thereby eliminating the conflict. However, the teacher looked at the situation as one that offered an opportunity to provide guided practice in how to make wise decisions. As the solution was implemented, feelings of caring and sharing were naturally reinforced.

This building of esprit de corps is especially useful in helping troubled students. A student, other than one who may have severe problems, will indeed find it difficult to hold out against peers, teachers, the principal, and parents/guardians. Also, the Support Group will provide help to the troubled student and his or her teacher. Most of all, don't give up! Focus hard for several weeks on positive recognition for wise decisions and on logical consequences for unwise decisions and be consistent. Reteach and guide practice.

If You Begin to Think: "The Program Does Not Work with My Kids"

The Positive Discipline philosophy and techniques will work if you work the plan. Review the flowchart shown in Figure 2–1 and the material in Chapter 4. Also, check the time lines for each week to be sure you didn't forget to do something critical.

When Your Class Has a Substitute Teacher

A sample Substitute Review Form is included at the end of this chapter. The one-day substitute can be an important public relations person in your community. If he or she is impressed with your program in one day, the individual will talk about it. Handouts from this guide should be given to the long-term substitute to help sustain the program. It is comforting to know discipline is in place and the classroom is running smoothly while you are absent.

Keeping Positive Discipline Exciting and Motivating for Students

Team Members (Achievers)

The team members need some periodic incentives to keep them monitoring and correcting their own decision making. They need to know that they are appreciated and that they are doing a good job.

Consider a special incentive cycle to supplement Classroom Team Time. Every three or four weeks should be sufficient because students receive weekly recognition in the classroom through Team Time and enjoy special privileges almost daily. You may wish to adjust the cycle during certain times of the year. For example, more frequent team activities during the last weeks of school are often desirable.

Here is a list of possible special recognition activities and incentives. Add your own ideas to the list.

- Display names on a hall bulletin board or in the office.
- Provide letters to the family about the success of the student in making good decisions.
- Provide a small concrete reward like a bookmark or a stick of gum.
- Arrange for a special assembly or get-together for team members. Activities could include a sing-a-long, special speaker or guest, or student performances.
- Provide printed membership cards to carry in wallets.
- Provide printed cards for parents to carry in wallets.
- Arrange for special recognition with parents and the principal when your whole room maintains membership for a month. This should be a special occasion.
- Teach a classroom team cheer or chant. Sample cheers and chants are included in the appendix.

Almost Achievers

After several weeks of effort, this group may profit from small group sessions with the teacher or counselor if one is available to assist. It is suggested these sessions be held periodically. Increased involvement can bring almost immediate progress.

At the meetings offer congratulations to those making improvement. Next, provide time for those students who are willing to share behaviors that are no longer a problem. Then ask about behaviors that are still causing problems and seek group suggestions. Express that you know they are trying and that you know they may sometimes be discouraged. Share some of the events in your life that have meant a great deal to you but that took tremendous effort. Share your belief in the students' ultimate achievement. Providing some extra encouragement and support may be just what students need to achieve success. Remember: Virtually all students can achieve if given adequate instruction, time, and support.

Students Working with a Support Group

Close contact should be maintained with Support Group members by sharing the ups and downs. Support Group maintenance need not be time-consuming. The teacher needs to meet the student for private weekly conferences. Your actions could include any of the following:

- Encourage the student to verbalize what has gone well.
- Verbalize how you see the student's progress.
- Award mini-recognitions for progress.
- Document progress together. A picture of a staircase may serve to visually show a student that reaching any goal is a series of small steps. A simple chart kept in the student's desk might be helpful.

As one author worked with a problem student, together they designed a chart that was taped to the inside of the student's desk top. The chart was simple. The author helped the student remember to mark the chart at scheduled times. As the student began to make slow progress, she had the added encouragement of a concrete picture of the progress. The chart seemed to be the one single factor that most helped this student become successful.

New Students Entering the Classroom

Orientation of new students needs to be carefully planned. The teacher informs the newcomers of the expectations, explains the team, and discusses the advantages of being a member of the team. It is usually helpful to appoint one or two buddies to help the teacher orient new students and teach them about behavior. Students are then given two to three weeks to practice the expectations. One of the privileges of team membership can be to act as a buddy to new students. When the new students' actions warrant, they may be admitted to the club.

Review Lessons

Occasionally, during the year, you will need to review expectations and the concept of esprit de corps. You would never go several weeks without a lesson in reading or math; similarly, you will not want to let several weeks go by without an occasional lesson in Positive Discipline. Lessons in the appendix will help you get started in the planning of review lessons.

Keeping Positive Discipline Exciting and Motivating for Parents/Guardians

Parents/guardians have been supportive in those schools currently using Positive Discipline. Your parents/guardians will support the program if you communicate regularly about the progress of your program. Anything you do with children is carried to the community. Your sense of pride and excitement will be felt. Here are some ideas:

- Write an article for the school newspaper about your activities.
- Provide personal letters to parents when a child receives team membership.
- Describe the program at Open House or at parent/teacher conferences.
- Show off team memberships on bulletin boards outside the classroom.
- Encourage PTA groups or parent organizations to provide support, money, and/or incentives.
- Provide parents/guardians of achievers the opportunity to present a library book to the school in honor of their child's achievement.
- Provide parents with a card or insert for possible inclusion in letters to grandparents, uncles, aunts, and so on.

Sample Parent/Guardian Letter 1: "Introducing Positive Discipline"

To:

From:

Subject: Positive Discipline

This year I am using a new discipline plan called Positive Discipline. The program is focused on guiding students toward assuming responsibility for their own behavior and toward becoming self-disciplined. I believe they will learn skills that will foster lifelong success. They will be learning to make appropriate decisions and choices in four areas: achievement, interactions, safety, and surroundings.

It is my belief and my goal that virtually all of my students will achieve success if they are provided with appropriate instruction, time for practice, and support. Your help is needed with the instruction and support. A sense of peer support will be developed in the classroom to help sustain the growth of Positive Discipline throughout the year.

Expectations that are taught to students form the basic core of an effective classroom. Inappropriate decisions and choices will be followed by logical rather than punitive consequences. Students will receive recognition and privileges for growth in Positive Discipline, including membership in our classroom team. As skills are learned, the potential for academic growth is enhanced. I hope you will soon be informed that your child has accepted the responsibility to make appropriate decisions at school that will support growth in Positive Discipline.

I will be communicating with you frequently concerning your child's progress. Attached is a list of our classroom expectations. The students helped determine these expectations. Please review the list with your child and call me with any questions or concerns.

(*Note to the Teacher:* A list of your classroom expectations needs to be attached to this letter.)

Sample Letter 2:
"Positive Discipline Achiever"

Dear _____,

    Congratulations! _____ is successfully demonstrating responsibility for appropriate classroom behavior and is making appropriate decisions about achievement, interactions, safety, and surroundings.

    _____ will receive recognition for his/her achievement_____at_____ in the _____. You are invited to share in this occasion by attending the ceremony or by recognizing _____'s achievement in your own way at home.

_____
    Teacher

Sample Parent Letter 3:
"Positive Discipline Progress"

To:

From:

Subject: Progress in Positive Discipline

    Several weeks ago you received my letter about our Positive Discipline plan. I am happy to report that _____ is making progress toward our classroom goals.

    The checklist below shows areas of growth and progress, as well as areas where additional growth is needed. As you can see, progress is being made and I feel _____ will soon meet the criteria as a Positive Discipline Achiever.

	Is Achieving	Is Making Progress
Achievement	_____	_____
Interactions	_____	_____
Safety	_____	_____
Surroundings	_____	_____

Comments: _____

_____

_____

Sample Elementary School Substitute Review Form

WELCOME TO OUR CLASSROOM!

A special program, Positive Discipline, is used in this classroom. These students are responsible for making good decisions about achievement, interactions, surroundings, and safety. I do not expect students to be perfect, but I do expect them to respond positively if you ask them to stop a behavior or to do something for you. Our expectations are posted. Please read them. As with everyone else, children like to know they're doing a good job. If you feel they are doing a good job, let them know several times throughout the day.

I am pleased to have you in our classroom and hope you enjoy your day. A folder of pertinent information will be found on the desk. All staff members are willing to help. The teachers in the adjoining rooms are acquainted with my room procedures. At the end of the day, please respond to the following:

1. Did you find information and materials adequate for your teaching responsibilities?

2. What could I have done to make your day more pleasant and successful?

3. How did you feel about the behavior of the students?

4. Any additional comments?

Thank you!

_____ _____
Signature of Substitute   Date

ALL-SCHOOL DESIGN

CHAPTER 6

Orienting a Staff to Positive Discipline

Chapters 6 through 9 are addressed to those who wish to implement Positive Discipline in the school as a whole. Usually, the principal leads, but any member of the staff may take the leadership role as long as the principal is in full agreement and willing to play an active role in all aspects of the program.

One of the big tasks in an all-school implementation is to help the staff understand the Positive Discipline philosophy and to begin to function as teachers of self-discipline instead of controllers of students. This is a big step to be taken by those who are truly interested in applying Positive Discipline and empowering students to make decisions about their behavior. Chapter 6 is a step-by-step guide designed to help begin the process of philosophical change.

Assessment

Before beginning an all-school Positive Discipline program, review the materials in Chapter 3. Select techniques and/or surveys to use. The authors encourage use of at least some of the materials suggested because you will be building commitment to a change process. People are more willing to change what they have helped determine needs to be changed. They are less likely to become involved in any change effort when they have had no part in determining a need for change.

The flowchart presented earlier in this book has been adapted for use in an all-school plan. The basic plan is the same but subtle changes reflect the involvement of teachers and students in developing the program for an entire school. See Figure 6–1.

Orienting the Staff

Orienting your staff is one of the most important steps you will take towards implementing a successful Positive Discipline program at your school.

As we said earlier, this is your opportunity to explain to your staff the Positive Discipline approach, emphasizing the features that address problems identified in the needs assessment. As the staff begins to understand what Positive Discipline can do for your school, you will be well on your way to building a school group who will enthusiastically participate in implementing the program.

Make sure you are well prepared. First, review Chapters 1 and 2, several times if necessary. Next, complete a needs assessment and have the results ready to present (see Chapter 3). As an alternative, you may wish to present the Positive Discipline program for staff approval before conducting a needs assessment. In this way your staff can get involved in gathering information, conducting surveys, and so on, once they agree to proceed with implementation and understand how the results will be used.

Then review the Staff Orientation outline in this chapter for use just as it is, or modify the presentation to suit your situation. Announce the orientation meeting well in advance. Make as many copies of the handouts as you need (all of them are at the end of this chapter) and get the meeting room ready, making certain that there will be enough seats for everyone.

The staff orientation will take approximately two hours. The orientation can be broken into a series of shorter staff meetings if necessary. There are advantages and disadvantages to both approaches. In a one-session approach, the staff gets a total picture in the space of a few hours. In the series-of-meetings approach, the principal can allow time for the material to be absorbed, for the staff to discuss portions, and/or for clarification of ideas.

Sample Staff Orientation Outline

(Notes and instructions to the leader appear in parentheses in italic printing.)

Figure 6–1. All-School Flowchart

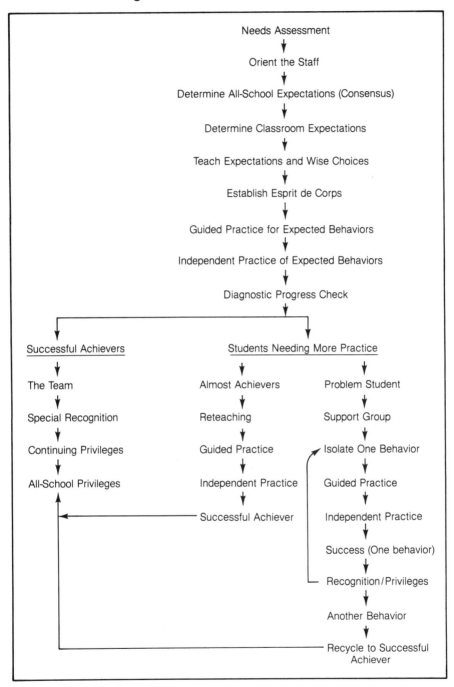

Needs Assessment

Orient the Staff

Determine All-School Expectations (Consensus)

Determine Classroom Expectations

Teach Expectations and Wise Choices

Establish Esprit de Corps

Guided Practice for Expected Behaviors

Independent Practice of Expected Behaviors

Diagnostic Progress Check

Successful Achievers	Students Needing More Practice	
The Team	Almost Achievers	Problem Student
Special Recognition	Reteaching	Support Group
Continuing Privileges	Guided Practice	Isolate One Behavior
All-School Privileges	Independent Practice	Guided Practice
	Successful Achiever	Independent Practice
		Success (One behavior)
		Recognition/Privileges
		Another Behavior
		Recycle to Successful Achiever

Welcome and Introduction

Thank you all for coming. Our needs assessment of school discipline indicates the majority of you would like to see an all-school discipline plan that is focused on teaching students self-discipline and that recognizes students who behave and make decisions about themselves and others appropriately.

(Your actual needs as identified in the needs assessment may be inserted here.)

There is a new plan that appears to offer some real help in the area of school discipline. It is one in which students are recognized for wise decision making and appropriate behavior. It requires little record keeping and offers a helping hand to teachers with difficult kids and classes. Schools in which the program has been used are reporting good acceptance by students, staff, and the community. It is called Positive Discipline.

I would like to review this program with you to see if it might meet the needs we have identified in our needs assessment.

Philosophy

(Distribute Handout 1: Philosophy.)

The philosophy of the Positive Discipline program is based on: "Virtually all students can and will master the skills needed to function appropriately in the school community if given adequate instruction, sufficient time, and support."

Positive Discipline is based on the belief that virtually all students can be taught to make appropriate decisions about their own and others' well-being virtually all the time. The program builds on this philosophy by helping the school staff provide direct instruction in the skills that students need to make appropriate decisions about individual achievement, interactions with others, safety, and surroundings. The school staff develops behavioral expectations and decision-making skills that are explained, taught, and practiced. Positive consequences are established for appropriate behavior and decisions, including recognition and privileges. These are balanced by reteaching and/or planning, and by using logical rather than punitive consequences for inappropriate behavior or when students' decisions are not in their best interest. Clear expectations and consequences guide students in their decisions as they learn the skills needed for life-long success. Within this structured framework, the staff builds a caring climate that fosters students' growth in self-discipline and personal responsibility.

All-School Flowchart—Part I

(Distribute Handout 2: Flowchart.)

This flowchart outlines the Positive Discipline program and shows the sequence of events to be followed in implementing the program and making it work. I would like to walk you through it step-by-step and explain each item as we go along.

(Direct attention to "Needs Assessment.")

To begin, we have assessed (or will assess) our discipline needs. We will use the results during the planning process.

(Direct attention to "Orient the Staff.")

To develop an all-school program, it is important for everyone to help determine the details of the program for our school. Therefore, this step is recommended.

(Direct attention to "Determine All-School Expectations (Consensus).")

We would develop all-school expectations for behavior. These would be the major behavioral standards we would have for every school child and we would all teach and recognize them consistently. Here are some examples of all-school expectations from two other schools.

(Distribute Handout 3A: All-School Expectations—1. Read through and discuss some of the examples.)

Can you think of some all-school expectations that might work for us? Can you add to this sample list?

(Write down suggestions from the staff.)

(Distribute Handout 3B: All-School Expectations—2.)

Some schools choose to agree on more specific behavior for the various public areas of the school including the hall and restroom. Here is a sample for you to consider. We will discuss this possibility later.

(Distribute Handout 4: Four Areas of Decisions.)

Four decision-making areas are stressed in Positive Discipline. In general, making appropriate decisions is really what a happy, productive life is all about. As children or adults we are constantly called upon to make decisions about these four areas.

(Distribute Handout 5: Achievement.)

Here are some typical decisions we make or have made in the area of achievement. For adults this might include going to college, chairing a town committee, or going to work everyday. For children, the decisions could include getting good grades, working hard at school, becoming an Eagle Scout, and so forth. Can you think of some others to add to this list?

(Write down suggestions from the staff.)

(Distribute Handout 6: Interactions.)

Interactions is the area that includes how we relate to others and to respecting the rights of others. For adults this could include making appropriate decisions about caring for family members, developing and sustaining friendships, and contributing to the community. For children it involves getting along without fighting and being aware of the rights of others. Can you think of some others to add to this list?

(Write down suggestions from the staff.)
(Distribute Handout 7: Safety.)

This area deals with the decisions we make to keep us physically safe and healthy. Either as children or adults we constantly make decisions where we, hopefully, say no to dangerous or harmful things. We decide to eat sensibly and exercise. We drive safely and obey traffic laws. Students need to choose to use playground equipment safely, walk instead of run in the halls, and fasten their seat belts. This is personal citizenship. Can you think of some others to add to this list?

(Write down suggestions from the staff.)
(Distribute Handout 8: Surroundings.)

This area deals with care and decision making about our environment. It is citizenship in the group sense. For example, as teachers, we take care of and use AV equipment properly. Children need to decide to take care of their own and school property. Can you think of some others to add to this list?

(Write down suggestions from the staff.)
(Refer staff to Handout 4: Four Areas of Decisions, once again.)

As we talked about these four areas, you noticed we related them to adults as well as to students. What we are going to be teaching our students with Positive Discipline is decision-making skills they will use throughout their lives. That seems to make this program especially worthwhile. Before we go on to other areas of this program, share with me some discipline problems you have recently experienced and let's see if they fit in one of the four areas. (Authors' note: Believe us, everything will fit!)

(Refer staff to Handout 2: Flowchart, again. Direct attention to "Determine Classroom Expectations.")

Within a classroom, each individual teacher determines classroom guidelines. You and your students would work out expectations for your room together.

(Direct attention to "Teach Expectations and Wise Choices.")

The staff actually teaches the students lessons on how to successfully meet behavioral expectations and how to make decisions that are in the best interest of students. These lessons would be taught in the same way that effective lessons in math or reading are taught. Sample lessons are provided in the program.

The Teaching Model

(Distribute Handout 9: The Teaching Model.)
Positive Discipline uses a structured teaching model to develop sample lessons. It can help us teach lessons on behavior and decision making in the same way we teach lessons in reading and math. The model can be used at all grade levels and can be easily adapted to fit your particular teaching style. Briefly, the model contains ten steps.
(Direct attention to "Focus.")
The first step in a Positive Discipline lesson is a "focus" designed to bring attention to the lesson. A focus gets the mental and physical attention of the students.
(Direct attention to "Rationale.")
A rationale or reason for learning the expectation is then given. We as adults respond to expectations far better when we know why. Valid reasons for expectations also help students understand.
(Direct attention to "Objective.")
The objective is stated and/or written in measurable and behavioral terms so students know exactly what they must do to demonstrate mastery of the expectation.
(Direct attention to "Input" then "Model.")
The teacher provides instructional input or information needed to accomplish the objective and offers a model of the finished product.
(Direct attention to "Guided Practice.")
Next, the teacher carefully monitors and recognizes the behaviors learned, then, during guided practice, gives students several opportunities to master the objective.
(Direct attention to "Independent Practice.")
Opportunities to practice expected behaviors on their own are provided during independent practice.
(Direct attention to "Diagnostic Progress Check.")
A diagnostic progress check is developed and the teacher assesses progress toward mastery.
(Direct attention to "Correctives" then "Extensions.")
Finally, the teacher provides correctives for those students not yet achieving mastery and extensions for those who have dem-

onstrated mastery. Correctives are additional learning experiences provided by the teacher and extensions are opportunities for students to apply their newly learned skills.

The philosophy of the Positive Discipline program states that virtually all children can and will learn to behave appropriately given adequate instruction, sufficient time, and support. The behaviors we as a staff decide our students should be taught could be presented using this teaching model. The program contains lesson plans for your use. These plans could be used just as they are or you could choose to use other approaches.

All-School Flowchart—Part II

(Refer staff to Handout 2: Flowchart, again. Direct attention to "Establish Esprit de Corps.")

One thing that makes Positive Discipline unique is the esprit de corps developed by the teacher and the students in the classroom. This is a key component of the program.

In order to develop self-discipline, students need the support and approval of their classmates as they learn to make wise decisions. Sample lessons provided for the teacher aid the development of a caring, supporting classroom atmosphere.

(Distribute Handout 10: Esprit de Corps. First discuss only the top half: Part I—"Achievers and Nonachievers." Direct attention to "Nonachievers.")

Many times students are isolated by their own deviant behavior. The more teachers and classmates get disgusted, the more the misfit is obligated to retaliate. Self-concept goes down and a vicious cycle of unacceptable behaviors results.

(Now discuss the bottom half: Part II—"Achievers, Nonachievers, Staff.")

In order to break this vicious cycle, the program provides activities to build esprit de corps in the classroom. Esprit de corps is a French term meaning "spirit of the group." Esprit de corps is present in a group when every member feels cared for and included, and willingly supports efforts toward group goals. In essence, with the development of esprit de corps, the classroom becomes much like an effective family unit.

Part II is a diagram of how esprit de corps helps break a behavioral cycle. The nonachiever is literally in the middle of things and is being supported by staff and other students. Sample lessons on developing esprit de corps or a feeling of family support are included in the Positive Discipline program.

Achievers become an active part of a classroom program to help the nonachiever make progress. The amount and kinds of classroom privileges for the whole class depend on steady progress of the nonachiever and continued good decision making by all class members.

(Refer staff to Handout 2: Flowchart, again. Direct attention to "Guided Practice for Expected Behaviors.")

We would provide students time to practice expected behaviors and wise decision making, giving them guidance, making suggestions, and providing positive recognition. We would also develop and provide reteaching and/or logical consequences for unwise decisions when needed. Guided practice might take three to four weeks.

(Direct attention to "Independent Practice of Expected Behaviors.")

Just as we provide practice time on math skills without direct teacher assistance, we would give students time to practice expected behaviors and practice consistently wise decisions or decisions in their own best interest. Independent practice would mean a chance to make decisions about personal behaviors that meet school and classroom expectations. The time line for this phase is one to two weeks.

(Direct attention to "Diagnostic Progress Check.")

At this point the teacher divides the students into two groups: successful achievers and students needing more practice. We would rely on teacher judgment as to which students are placed into each group.

(Direct attention to "Successful Achievers.")

The students identified as successful achievers receive special recognition and become eligible for school-wide privileges and certain other privileges in the classroom.

(Direct attention to "The Team.")

As students become proficient (not necessarily perfect) at making appropriate decisions about their behavior, they generally become self-correcting. When this happens, they are recognized as wise decision makers by being awarded special recognition and privileges.

The Positive Discipline program suggests a school team. Students are awarded certificates, buttons, or similar symbols of their membership. We would need to decide together on a team name. One school group named their club the "Royal Knights"; another group chose the "Golden Treasure Team." A mascot could also be used as a school team name. Perhaps more importantly, we would need to determine together what privileges members would receive. For example, we might decide that only team members could serve on the Student Council. Maybe we could decide that only team members would be eligible for special activities during the noon recess, or think of other activities and privileges that fit our students. We will also decide together how to determine eligibility for the team.

(Direct attention to "Students Needing More Practice.")

Two distinct groups are left. The first group contains those students who have almost met the expectations, the "Almost Achievers." They are learning, working, and trying. These students are provided some reteaching, more guided and independent practice, and one by one join the Successful Achiever group.

(Direct attention to "Problem Student.")

The second group contains the problem students. At some point a teacher may want to say, "I have a problem student. This student needs more help than I am able to give."

(Direct attention to "Support Group.")

At this time a Support Group is used. The classroom teacher, principal, parent, counselor, a favorite teacher, or a student might all become a part of the support system to encourage the non-achiever, working together to help the student learn to make appropriate decisions about behavior. This is done by isolating one behavior at a time. The Support Group can be a real lifeline for the teacher. Some nonachievers may be candidates for special education, but most children who are failing in their social interactions are not. They are merely kids who feel they are "misfits" and are often excluded by their own behaviors.

In order to help the problem student make progress toward team membership, one measurable behavior at a time is selected for improvement. With esprit de corps working in the classroom and with the Support Group encouraging improvement on one measurable behavior at a time, almost 100 percent of the students make progress. They don't become perfect, but they do make progress. The Support Group works on one behavior at a time, recycling as necessary through guided practice, independent practice, mini-privileges, and recognition until this special student also becomes a Successful Achiever.

The Support Group approach need not be time-consuming. It is simply one or more people other than the teacher saying, "Here is the one thing you need to improve on. We know you can. We'll help you any way we can and we'll really be happy for you when you achieve this goal."

(Direct attention to "Determine All-School Expectations (Consensus)" near the top of the flowchart.)

That brings us back to something that was mentioned earlier in this orientation: Consensus.

The tasks ahead include deciding whether or not to adopt a

Positive Discipline program, what parts of the program might work best for us, and what parts we might want to delete.

If we do decide to adopt Positive Discipline, then we will need to decide on all-school expectations, talk about classroom expectations, and learn more about teaching expectations and wise decision making by using the Teaching Model. We will also have to learn more about establishing esprit de corps, determining all-school privileges, and so forth. Let's begin with your questions and concerns.

(Answer questions from the staff and take notes.)

Conclusion

Thank you all for coming and participating with so much enthusiasm! I believe we decided to _____. *(Insert actions the group has decided to take next, for example, a second meeting, conduct a needs assessment, survey, etc.)*

Note to the leader: At this point you may need to provide only general support, or your staff may still need quite a few specifics. Only you know whether you need to zero in immediately for implementation action or whether your staff needs time to think, talk, and discuss the subject. We urge you not to implement Positive Discipline until a clear majority concurs and any minority group commits to a definite trial period.

Positive Discipline Philosophy

Virtually all students can and will master the skills needed to function appropriately in the school community if given adequate instruction, sufficient time, and support.

Handout 2: All-School Flowchart

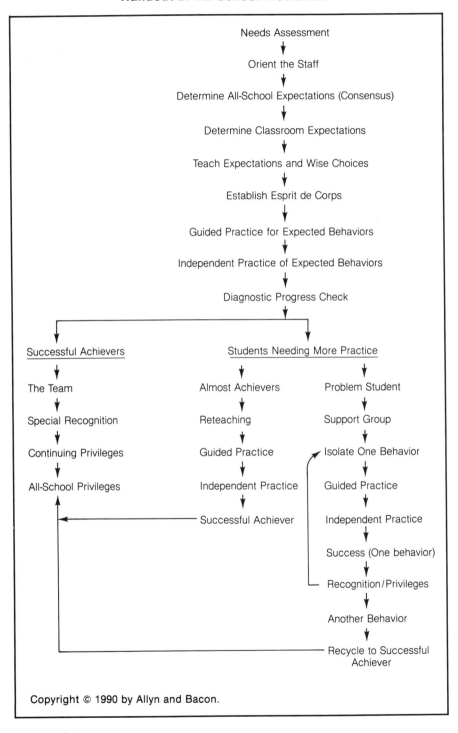

Needs Assessment
↓
Orient the Staff
↓
Determine All-School Expectations (Consensus)
↓
Determine Classroom Expectations
↓
Teach Expectations and Wise Choices
↓
Establish Esprit de Corps
↓
Guided Practice for Expected Behaviors
↓
Independent Practice of Expected Behaviors
↓
Diagnostic Progress Check

Successful Achievers
↓
The Team
↓
Special Recognition
↓
Continuing Privileges
↓
All-School Privileges

Students Needing More Practice

Almost Achievers
↓
Reteaching
↓
Guided Practice
↓
Independent Practice
↓
Successful Achiever

Problem Student
↓
Support Group
↓
Isolate One Behavior
↓
Guided Practice
↓
Independent Practice
↓
Success (One behavior)
↓
Recognition / Privileges
↓
Another Behavior
↓
Recycle to Successful Achiever

School A

Be kind.
Work hard.

School B

Work and play hard.
Be safe.
Respect self and others.
Respect property.

Philosophy

We believe that virtually all students can and will master the skills needed to function appropriately in the school community if given adequate instruction, sufficient time, and support. Students are expected to be responsible for making appropriate decisions and choices about achievement, surroundings, interactions, and safety.

All-School Expectations

- Leave personal space.
- Keep hands, feet, and objects to self.
- Help keep the school clean and in good repair.
- Use only words that help others feel OK.
- Carry out the reasonable requests of all adults.
- Choose not to fight.
- Use a pass when outside the classroom.
- Gum, candy, snacks only with teacher permission and supervision.

Classroom Expectations

- The teacher is in charge. He or she will explain what is expected.
- Know your classroom expectations and do what your teacher says.
- Know the expectations for gym, music, and library.
- Do what the teacher says.

Bicycle Expectations

- Park in the bicycle racks.
- Walk bikes to and from the street.
- Know and follow city bike laws.

Arrival/Departure Expectations

- Arrive on time—between 8:50 and 9:00 a.m.
- Cross streets only when patrol is on duty.
- Carry out all reasonable requests of patrol members.
- Leave the school grounds promptly after school.
- Sign in or out of the office if you arrive late or leave early.

Hall Expectations

- Leave personal space.
- Keep hands, feet, and objects to self.
- Move quietly; don't disturb others.
- Walk on the right side.

(continued)

Handout 3B: All-School Expectations—2 (*continued*)

Restroom Expectations

- Keep walls and floors clean.
- Use quiet voices.
- Put trash in containers.
- Use supplies wisely.

Assembly Expectations

- Listen courteously during the program.
- Show appropriate appreciation.
- Leave personal space.
- Keep hands, feet, and objects to self.

Lunchroom/Lunch Line Expectations

- Leave personal space.
- Keep hands, feet, objects, and food to self.
- Use quiet voices.
- No talking when lights are out.
- Sit in assigned place.
- Leave assigned place only with permission.

Achievement

Interactions

Safety

Surroundings

Achievement

Adults	*Children*
College Volunteer Go to Work	Get Good Grades Work Hard at School Become Eagle Scout

Interactions

Adults	*Children*
Care for Family Members Develop and Sustain Friendships Contribute to Community	Get Along without Fighting Awareness of Rights of Others

Safety

Adults	*Children*
Exercise	Use
Eat	School
Sensibly	Equip-
Obey	ment
Traffic	Walk in
Laws	Hall
	Fasten
	Seat Belt

Surroundings

Adults	*Children*
Share AV Equip- ment Care of Home and Work Environ- ment	Care of Property Eat Politely

Teaching Model

Focus
Rationale
Objective
Input
Model
Guided Practice
Independent Practice
Diagnostic Progress Check
Correctives
Exensions

Esprit de Corps

I:

(Achievers) | Nonachievers |

II:

Achievers

(Nonachievers)

Staff

CHAPTER 7

Planning for All-School Implementation

Once the leader has introduced the staff to Positive Discipline in an orientation session and the staff has agreed to implement the program, the leader needs to set aside some additional time for the staff to reach consensus on how the process will work and to define the specifics of the program for the school. The leader will also need to provide further details and clarify several aspects of the program that have been only briefly described to the staff at this point. Frequently the leader is the principal; however, any highly respected member of the staff could lead the staff in all-school implementation. Perhaps the leadership could be shared by the principal and other staff members who are effective group leaders. Regardless of who leads, the principal must play a very active role in the implementation process.

It will probably take about two hours to cover the following agenda, possibly longer. The session can be broken up into shorter meetings if necessary. Planning for implementation is important—the time and effort invested in ironing out the details and resolving any anticipated difficulties is well worth it. Good planning will make running the program much easier in the long run. The leader's role is time-consuming at this point. However, once established, the program requires very little time to sustain. In fact, most of the ongoing time spent on the program is pleasant, since everyone's role becomes one of emphasizing and recognizing the appropriate and wise decisions made by students.

You and your staff have probably established effective ways of working together on similar tasks in the past. Whenever possible, use those familiar methods. They may provide shortcuts to accomplishing the necessary. A meeting agenda is helpful at this phase so that nothing is overlooked. Support materials are listed beside each agenda item along with their page location. You should have these materials copied prior to the meeting so materials can be distributed as each item is discussed. Encourage the staff to keep all the materials together in a notebook or file folder for future reference.

Agenda and Support Materials

Agenda	*Support Materials*
1. Define and reach consensus on All-School Expectations.	Key Concept 1: Determining Expectations (page 21) and All-School Expectations—1 and —2 (pages 149–151). Sample Classroom Expectations (pages 175–176).
2. Review procedures to establish Classroom Expectations.	
3. Review the Teaching Model.	Key Concept 2: The Teaching Model (pages 23–24).
4. Define and discuss what to do when students demonstrate appropriate behavior (choose wisely).	Key Concept 4: What to Do When Students Choose Wisely (pages 27–30).
5. Discuss the all-school team.	Key Concept 5: The Team (pages 31–34).
6. Define and discuss what to do when students demonstrate inappropriate behavior (choose unwisely).	Key Concept 6: What to Do When Students Choose Unwisely (pages 35–39); Silent Conferences (pages 177–180); What Happened? (page 178); What Is the Problem? (page 179); and Problem-Solving Sessions (pages 181–182).
7. Define and develop an understanding of Esprit de Corps.	Key Concept 3: Esprit de Corps (pages 25–26).
8. Define and discuss the support group.	Key Concept 7: The Support Group (pages 41–42); Problem Student Referral and Student Intervention Contract (pages 183–186).

9. Discuss involving and communicating with parents.
10. Discuss and resolve staff concerns.
11. Adjourn.

All-School Planning Meeting

Agenda Item 1: Define and reach consensus on All-School Expectations.

Support Materials: Key Concept 1: Determining Expectations (page 21) and All-School Expectations—1 and —2 (pages 149–151).

Before discussing this item, distribute the support materials. You used Handouts 3A and 3B: "All-School Expectations" during the staff orientation. It is best to reissue the handouts along with the "Key Concept 1: Determining Expectations" material for discussion. This may also be an excellent time to provide the suggested notebook for each staff member.

After allowing time for staff members to skim the support materials, call for a brainstorming session to get a list of desired all-school expectations (formerly known as school rules) for your school. You may already have a list of school rules from the previous year. In any case, explain that an all-school expectation is one the entire staff agrees to teach, reteach, and support consistently. You may want to group suggested expectations using Transparency 4: Four Areas of Decisions. Encourage a free flow of ideas but limit discussion for the moment, and don't permit elimination of any suggestions until the next step.

The material, "Key Concept 1" contains information critical at this stage. More specifically, once your staff has brainstormed, ask them to eliminate any expectations that (1) cannot be taught, monitored, and enforced consistently, (2) are not reasonable expectations for all grade levels, (3) cannot be stated positively so students will know what they are to do instead of what they are not to do, or (4) cannot be fully supported by every staff member.

Next, guide the group towards stating each expectation in specific behavioral terms. Only when teachers can easily see whether or not students are meeting the expectations can behavior be consistently monitored. Some examples of appropriately stated expectations are contained in the staff handouts.

Agenda Item 2: Define procedures to establish Classroom Expectations.

Support Materials: Sample Classroom Expectations (pages 175–176).

Distribute Determining Classroom Expectations. Explain to the staff that they, along with their students, will each determine the expectations in their own classrooms and that it is not necessary for everyone to have the same classroom expectations. Next, ask the staff to read the handout. Then ask if anyone would like to share statements of classroom expectations they have found useful in previous years. Finally, ask those who have successfully involved students in determining classroom rules to describe the procedures used and the results of using this process.

Agenda Item 3: Review the Teaching Model.	Support Materials: Key Concept 2: The Teaching Model (pages 23–24).

Distribute Key Concept 2: The Teaching Model. Explain again that successful implementation of Positive Discipline involves actually teaching expected behaviors much like teachers teach the concepts and skills of reading and math. Ask the staff to briefly review the model. If your staff is familiar with similar lesson-plan models you will only need to provide time for clarification or discussion at this point. If the model is entirely new to your staff, you may need to spend some time discussing each lesson-plan step and applying the steps to a familiar task like preparing students for the first fire drill of the year. Several actual teaching lessons are provided in the appendix if you need additional models to use for this discussion.

Agenda Item 4: Define and discuss what to do when students demonstrate appropriate behavior (choose wisely).	Support Materials: Key Concept 4: What to Do When Students Choose Wisely (pages 27–30).

Begin by distributing Key Concept 4: What to Do When Students Choose Wisely. Explain that in order to teach students self-discipline the staff will need to make a concerted effort to recognize and postively reinforce students' appropriate behavior as they teach expected behaviors. Review Key Concept 4. Involve the staff by asking them to list additional reward activities in the individual or small-group categories. Also ask teachers to describe what has happened in their classrooms in previous years when positive recognition was used.

Agenda Item 5: Discuss the all-school team.	Support Materials: Key Concept 5: The Team (pages 31–34).

Next, ask the staff to thoroughly read Key Concept 5: The Team. Explain that most decisions concerning the team can wait until later. At this point they just need to have a general idea about how the team might work. They will want to let students know a team will be formed. The idea is to provide plenty of recognition and positive reinforcement for students who develop self-discipline.

Expect some concern about students not wanting to become team members. In the authors' experience, all students have desired team membership at some point in time. We've seen even the most resistant boys and girls work hard to earn team membership especially when they have been given appropriate support and encouragement.

Agenda Item 6: Define and discuss what to do when students demonstrate inappropriate behavior (choose unwisely).	Support Materials: Key Concept 6: What to Do When Students Choose Unwisely (pages 35–39); Silent Conferences (pages 177–180); What Happened? (page 178); What Is the Problem? (page 179); and Problem-Solving Sessions (pages 181–182).

Distribute Key Concept 6. Announce that although using positive recognition and reinforcement for appropriate behavior is critical to the success of the program, knowing effective techniques to use for inappropriate behavior is also necessary. Ask the staff to read the handout and explain that none of the recommended techniques are new to most teachers, but a quick review of effective techniques is needed.

Explain that Positive Discipline stresses the use of logical rather than punitive consequences for inappropriate behavior. Logical consequences are directly related to the student's behavior, delivered with a tone of regret, and carefully explained to the student. Discuss any aspects of the handout the staff wishes to cover. Encourage them to relate previous situations and personal experiences.

Next distribute "Silent Conferences" (pages 177–180). Explain that this technique is one way to address misbehavior in an inconspicuous and relatively nonconfrontive way. It is also a technique that minimizes teacher time involved and/or potential disruption to the normal flow of learning. Review the handouts and ask staff members how this technique and the forms might work for them.

Finally, distribute Problem-Solving Sessions (pages 181–182). The Problem-Solving Session handout is another technique recommended by the authors to deal with inappropriate behavior. Ask the group to skim the materials. Some teachers may have used similar techniques. If so, ask them to share their experiences.

Agenda Item 7: Define and develop an understanding of Esprit de Corps.	Support Materials: Key Concept 3: Esprit de Corps (pages 25–26).

Distribute and read aloud Key Concept 3: Esprit de Corps. Explain that the authors have included ten fully developed lesson plans to aid the staff in teaching esprit de corps and that the lessons are adaptable to any grade level. Ask the staff to comment on the handout.

Agenda Item 8: Define and discuss Students Needing More Practice.

Support Materials: Key Concept 7: The Support Group (pages 41–42); Problem Student Referral (page 183); and Student Intervention Contract (pages 185–186).

Distribute the support materials. Read the first paragraph of Key Concept 7 aloud. Ask the staff to review the remainder of the materials silently. Explain that the two forms included are only suggested forms that can be revised to suit the staff. Also, emphasize that the process involved need not take a lot of time and will be specifically designed for each student involved. Only the most difficult students will need the Support Group approach.

Agenda Item 9: Discuss involving and communicating with parents.

The program materials include sample news articles, letters to parents, and certificates that can be used at appropriate times during implementation. Describe these items briefly and then ask the staff how they might like to further involve the parents. For example, they may wish to inform parents when a child begins working with a Support Group. Parents may want to know why their child hasn't become a member of the team during the first one or two inductions. You and the staff will need to discuss possibilities and decide on your approach.

Agenda Item 10: Discuss and resolve staff concerns.

Ask the staff to voice any concerns they may have at this point. Encourage open and honest discussion. Indicate that the program provides a suggested time line for the first few weeks of implementation that can be used as is or modified to fit the situation. Also explain that the program contains many support materials, including lesson plans for each week in the time line. You might choose to distribute these items with a Positive Discipline Bulletin each week.

Agenda Item 10: Adjourn.

Close by thanking your staff for their willingness to support the group's efforts so far and for their commitment to work towards developing self-disciplined students who possess the skills needed for life-long success.

Support Materials

Various support materials can be found at the end of this chapter and in the appendix.

Suggested Readings

Glasser, William, *Schools Without Failure* (New York: Harper and Row Publishers, Inc., 1969), pages 122–185.

Nelsen, Jane, *Positive Discipline: Teaching Children Self-Discipline, Responsibility, Cooperation and Problem-Solving Skills* (Fair Oaks, CA: Sunrise Press, 1981), pages 99–118.

Sample Classroom Expectations

Expectations or rules differ from one classroom to another. Each teacher is aware of how classroom discipline works best for his or her group of students. It is highly recommended that students and teachers decide together what the expectations should be for their classroom. Students are willing to fulfill expectations they feel are necessary, ones they understand, and ones they have helped select.

Students are expected to know and follow all-school expectations and, for some, bus expectations. They are also required to follow expectations or rules established by other teachers (PE, library, music etc.). Therefore, the fewer expectations or rules posted for the classroom, the easier it becomes for students to follow them. As few as three expectations and as many as five are suggested for the teacher and students to develop. As with all-school expectations, classroom expectations need to be stated positively so students will know what they are expected to do instead of just what not to do. They also need to be stated behaviorally so all can see when students are behaving as expected. Some teachers may elect to have the classroom expectations be the same as the all-school expectations. Some typical classroom expectations are listed below as reference material for use prior to involving students in designing expectations for their own classroom.

Sample Classroom Expectations
(Decide on no more than five.)

- Use pass to leave room.
- Be recognized before talking.
- Raise hand to talk or get out of seat.
- One person at the pencil sharpener.
- Only two people out of desks at one time.
- Put assignments in labeled baskets.
- Stay on task.
- Use indoor voice.
- Keep desk and floor clean.
- Respect each other.
- Recognize teacher requests.
- Complete assignments.
- Have paper and pencil available.

(*continued*)

Sample Classroom Expectations (*continued*)

One way to involve students in selecting the expectations for a classroom is to set aside about thirty minutes for a meeting. During the meeting, the teacher can discuss the terms *rules* and *expectations*. The point should be made that only students can control their own behavior. The teacher does not have to be an enforcer of rules but can instead act as one whose role is to help students learn, practice, and follow expectations as they achieve self-discipline. The class, including the teacher, can then suggest expectations for the classroom that will help learning take place. The classroom group can use either a vote or a consensus procedure to select the three to five expectations for the classroom.

Silent Conferences

The purpose of holding a silent conference is to minimize the amount of teacher time involved and/or potential disruption to the normal flow of learning. It is a good technique to use when feeling levels are high, when students from other rooms are involved, and when time is short and you need to get on with lessons. It can be used for problems such as talking out or an argument between people (student and student or teacher and student.)

The "What Happened?" and the "What Is the Problem?" Silent Conferences

Ask the students who are involved to sit down. Supply them with pencils and papers and have them write down what happened and what they each did. You may also want them to write about what they could have done instead. (The authors suggest you keep a supply of the two forms included here.) Writing both what happened and what they each did will help children vent frustrations and get them to focus on the real problem. It will also save time for the teacher. (One can read a lot faster than listen.) After written information has been obtained, other data can quickly be gathered and a fair decision made. Students will have some very inventive spellings you may need to clarify. If students from other rooms are involved (especially after recess) be sure to let their teacher know their location. It is even possible to give students a "What Happened?" or a "What Is the Problem?" form and let them complete it in their own room.

The "Problem Solving" Silent Conference

Let's say you are having a problem with a student interrupting and talking without permission. Normally, this student is not a big problem, but today he is really getting to you. Grab a sheet of paper or a large filing card and start a silent conference. You can go right on with activities. On the paper or file card, explain your perception of the problem. For example, write:

> "John, today you are having trouble raising your hand before you talk. You do not usually have this trouble. What is the problem?"

(continued)

What Happened?

What did you do?

What could you have done instead?

178

What Is the Problem?

Name two great things about you.

What is the problem?

What do you need to do to solve the problem?

Will things be better for you when you solve the problem? How?

List the steps you will take to solve the problem.

Who will need to help you with the steps of your plan?

You need to keep track of your progress and reward yourself for progress every day. How will you do that?

What do you think the results of your plan will be?

Silent Conferences (*continued*)

Now, hand the paper to John. Encourage him, nonverbally, to write his answer on the paper. He might write:

"I don't know."

You then take the paper back and write:

"Can you get this under control?"

Again, hand the paper to John. He might write:

"Yes."

You then write:

"Good!"

Of course, this is a very simple example, but it should give you the general idea. Some teachers like to use a standard 4″ × 5″ card for silent conferences. They can be dated and kept in a card file for future reference.

Problem-Solving Sessions

Although lessons on common school problem areas (Conflict Resolution, Manage Your Fate, and Go with the Flow) are included in the appendix, no one can anticipate every problem any one class may have. Each class has a personality and accompanying problems of its own. Some groups are prone to lying, putting each other down, or rumor passing; others are not. Frequently it doesn't do much good to tell the class to stop. The authors encourage the reader to consult books by William Glasser and Jane Nelsen for detailed descriptions of class meetings. Techniques for such sessions can be invaluable as tools for changing difficult situations.

Classroom problem-solving sessions and classroom meetings can be helpful whenever a unique problem arises. A classroom problem-solving session involves setting aside twenty to thirty minutes of class time to discuss the problem, brainstorm solutions, and devise a system of evaluating progress toward correcting the problem. Begin by writing a clear statement of the problem on the board.

The following sample problem-solving outline will give you a good idea of how to get started on a problem-solving session:

Problem: _____

What's happening now?

What should be happening?

What needs to be done?

Who is going to do it?

Time line?

How will we know we're finished?

Using the outline above, the teacher asks students to help answer each question on the outline and writes the group's answers in the appropriate spaces. For example, a problem and possible solutions are outlined below.

(*continued*)

Problem-Solving Sessions (*continued*)

Problem: Name calling is causing a lot of our classmates to feel unhappy.

What's happening now?
There's too much name calling.

What should be happening?
Everyone should be saying only nice things about each other.

What needs to be done?
We need to say nothing at all if we can't say something nice.

Who is going to do it?
We are!

Time line?
One week.

How will we know we're finished?
No reports of name calling for one week.

Problem Student Referral

To:

From:

Student's Name:

The above named student is in need of additional support in his or her efforts to become self-disciplined. Please help us by attending a conference on _____ at _____ to discuss a target behavior and to help select the members of the Support Group.

Student Intervention Contract

Student's Name _____ Teacher _____ Room _____

Student Strengths _____
_____
_____

Team Members (3–5) _____ _____
                   _____ _____
                   _____

Target behavior:

Student's statement about what is to be done about the target behavior:

Recognition/Privileges to be provided for achievement:
_____
_____
_____

_____
 Student Signature

(Please see reverse side)

Teacher's Notes:

A. GUIDED PRACTICE
   Who guides practice? _____
   Checkpoint date(s): _____

B. INDEPENDENT PRACTICE
   Checkpoint date _____
   Teacher's evaluation of success _____
   _____
   _____

   _____   _____
        Date   Teacher Signature

CHAPTER 8

All-School Implementation

You and your staff are now ready to implement Positive Discipline with your students. The first few weeks will require the careful attention of everyone as the foundation for Positive Discipline is put in place. As the principal, or the person responsible for implementation, your task is to follow the guide. The needed materials are provided. Your experience will probably tell you which teachers will adapt easily and which will need encouragement or further support and instruction. In this chapter the authors provide a suggested overall time line, including weekly "bulletins," sample letters and news articles for parents, and some suggestions for involving classified staff members. Lesson plans for teachers are included in the appendix. Feel free to reorganize and develop your own time line or bulletins as you see fit. Approach implementation in the way that will work best for you.

There are a few things you should personally do during the first three weeks of implementation. The first three weeks are critical because they will set the tone and will likely determine the success of the program in your school.

First, be highly visible and act as an appropriate role model as you work with staff and students to teach and reinforce the lessons being taught. Provide an abundance of positive recognition to all.

Second, make numerous classroom visits to observe the process of teaching appropriate behavior and wise decision making. You may even wish to teach a few lessons yourself in order to emphasize the importance of the project.

Third, talk frequently and informally with individuals and small groups of staff members about their experiences, successes, and frustrations. Urge the staff to be realistic about the results of the first three weeks of work. Students are human and therefore imperfect—so is the staff. Although they can expect every student to behave properly virtually all of the time, on occasion students are likely to behave improperly. When this happens, as it surely will, encourage the staff to allow students to participate in the correction of their improper behavior. Even the most well-behaved student will need correction occasionally. Don't let the staff get discouraged. Remind them to assume students want to behave and get along. The staff is teaching students to regulate their own behavior, and before long they will.

Implementation Time Line

The following time line is suggested for the principal's use in monitoring implementation. Adjust the time line to meet your needs. Support materials for the principal are located at the end of this chapter and are numbered consecutively (1, 2, 3, etc.). Teacher support materials are located in the appendix. The materials you will need to distribute are ordered alphabetically (A, B, C, etc.). The authors recommend handing out only the items needed for one week at a time. Providing a notebook with the first week's materials helps teachers with organization.

Week 1

Principal Activities	*Principal Support Material*
• Prepare and distribute copies of weekly bulletin and teacher support material.	• Positive Discipline Bulletin—Week 1 (1) • See Teacher Support Materials below
• Provide students with recognition and logical consequences as occasions arise.	
• Send introduction letter to parents.	• Parent Letter—Program Begins (2)

Teacher Activities	*Teacher Support Materials*
• Introduce Positive Discipline.	• Introducing Positive Discipline (A)
• Determine and teach classroom expectations (no handout).	• Key Concept 1

- Teach and practice all-school expectations.
- Provide consistent recognition for success.
- Provide logical consequences for inappropriate behavior.
- Begin to build esprit de corps.
- Teach conflict resolution.
- Teach alternatives to fighting.
- Experiment with silent conferences

- Go with the Flow (B)
- Playground Expectations (C)
- Key Concept 4

- Key Concept 6.

- Esprit de Corps Lessons 1 & 2 (D & E)
- Conflict Resolution (F)
- Manage Your Fate (G)

- Pages 87–91

Week 2

Principal Activities

- Prepare and distribute copies of weekly bulletin and teacher support material.
- Include a Positive Discipline article in the school newsletter.
- Prepare copies of support materials.
- Continue to provide recognition and logical consequences.

Principal Support Materials

- Positive Discipline Bulletin—Week 2 (3)
- See Teacher Support Materials below.
- Sample News Article—"What's New?" (4)

- See Teacher Activities below.

Teacher Activities

- Review all expectations.
- Provide guided practice for all expectations.
- Continue to build esprit de corps.
- Introduce Classroom Problem Solving.
- Continue to provide recognition for success and logical consequences for inappropriate behavior.
- Discuss the School Team.

Teacher Support Materials

- Esprit de Corps Lessons 3, 4, 5 (H, I, J)
- Pages 181–182

Week 3

Principal Activities

- Prepare and distribute copies of weekly bulletin and teacher support material.
- Finalize details of the School Team.
- Include an article in the school newspaper.

- Prepare copies of support materials.
- Continue to provide recognition and logical consequences.

Principal Support Materials

- Positive Discipline Bulletin—Week 3 (5)
- See Teacher Support Materials below.
- Certificates and Sample Badges (6)
- Sample News Article—"New Achievement Group" (7)
- See Teacher Activities below.

Teacher Activities

- Review all expectations.
- Provide abundant guided practice.
- Provide abundant verbal recognition for success.
- Provide group recognition (Classroom Team Time) for progress.
- Provide logical consequences for inappropriate behavior.
- Continue to build esprit de corps.
- Hold a problem-solving session.
- Share new information about the School Team when available.

Teacher Support Materials

- Esprit de Corps Lesson 6 (K)

Week 4

Principal Activities

- Complete tasks for the Team.
- Prepare and distribute copies of weekly bulletin and teacher support material.

Principal Support Materials

- Positive Discipline Bulletin—Week 4 (8)
- See Teacher Support Materials below.

- Continue to provide recognition and logical consequences.
- Arrange for a "team time" for your staff. You might treat the staff to soft drinks or distribute awards or certificates. If everyone has been a "good egg," distribute hard-boiled eggs with a note thanking them for being "good eggs."

Teacher Activities

- Review expectations by using sponges.
- Teach new lessons.

- Provide recognition including Classroom Team Time and logical consequences.
- Continue to build esprit de corps.
- Introduce independent practice.

- Have students complete at least two self-analysis charts during the week.
- Diagnose students' progress by reviewing the self-analysis charts to see if you agree with the students or use a teacher checklist.
- Discuss specifics of the School Team.

Teacher Support Materials

- Positive Discipline Sponges (L).
- Brain Power (M)
- Staying on Task (N)
- Gossip (O)
- Making Choices (P)

- Esprit de Corps Lesson 7 (Q)
- Introducing Independent Practice (R) and Self-Analysis Charts (pages 281–288)

- Teacher Checklist (pages 289–290)

Week 5

Principal Activities

- Prepare and distribute copies of weekly bulletin.

Principal Support Materials

- Positive Discipline Bulletin—Week 5 (9)

- Discuss details of the support group with staff.
- Complete tasks for the School Team.
- Continue to provide recognition and logical consequences.

Teacher Activities
- Review expectations by using sponges.
- Provide recognition, Classroom Team Time, and logical consequences.
- Provide independent practice and extensions for qualified students.
- Have students complete self-analysis charts.
- Continue to diagnose student progress.
- Discuss the School Team.

Week 6

Principal Activities
- Prepare and distribute copies of weekly bulletin and teacher support material.
- Complete tasks for the School Team.
- Provide materials for support group and meet with students/teachers.
- Get lists of students who will make the team and prepare parent letters. Continue to provide recognition and logical consequences.
- Include an article in newsletter.

Principal Support Materials
- Positive Discipline Bulletin—Week 6 (10)
- See Teacher Support Materials below.

- Sample Parent Letter— Positive Discipline Achiever (11)

- Sample News Article— "School Team Begins" (12)

Teacher Activities

- Review expectations.
- Continue to provide recognition, logical consequences, guided and independent practice, and correctives/extensions.
- Prepare certificates for induction ceremony.
- List students needing more practice (two categories) for the principal.
- Meet with principal/ students on Support Group plans.
- Notify parents of nonachievers.

Teacher Support Materials

- Page 41–42

- Sample Letter—Positive Discipline Progress (S)

Week 7

Activities

- Prepare and distribute copies of weekly bulletin.
- Hold induction ceremony.
- Begin Intervention Plans.

Support Materials

- Positive Discipline Bulletin—Week 7 (13)

Notes Concerning Implementation

As you know, there is no one way to solve all discipline problems. By the time you and your staff have implemented the seven-week time line, you will need time to discuss perceptions. Consider rewarding yourselves with a fun activity. For example, plan a get-together with food and laughter during which you share the successes of the last few weeks. This will lead to discussing the adjustments that need to be made. Make plans to meet again to work on adjusting the program to suit your needs.

When the staff makes suggestions about how to adjust the program, you should encourage their creativity. Adapting the program to your individual situation is critical to your success. Your group is engaging in "fixing" their program rather than trying to "fix" students. What more can one ask?

Weekly Bulletins and Support Materials

Various support materials for this seven-week time line are included at the end of this chapter.

Positive Discipline Bulletin—Week 1 (1)

Teachers and Staff:

The authors of the Positive Discipline program strongly recommend concentrating on teaching behavior during the first three weeks of implementation. Consequently, do not expect to do as much as you usually do with academic subjects. Once self-discipline has been established, we can expect to go faster and further with academic subjects. In the long run we will save both time and effort.

You may need to review the Key Concepts and handouts discussed at the staff meeting when we planned for implementation. Please see me if you have misplaced any of your handouts—I have extras.

The suggested activities for this week as well as the next two are numerous, but I urge you do them thoroughly. You will find that the time and effort has been well spent. Please feel free to discuss any questions you have with me or your colleagues. Most of all, have some fun with the suggested activities this week!

(over)

Teacher Activities	Support Materials
• Introduce Positive Discipline.	• Introducing Positive Discipline (A)
• Determine and teach classroom expectations (no handout).	• Key Concept 1
• Teach and practice all-school expectations.	• Go with the Flow (B) • Playground Expectations (C)
• Provide consistent recognition for success.	• Key Concept 4
• Provide logical consequences for inappropriate behavior.	• Key Concept 6
• Begin to build esprit de corps.	• Esprit de Corps Lessons 1 & 2 (D & E)
• Teach conflict resolution.	• Conflict Resolution (F)
• Teach alternatives to fighting.	• Manage Your Fate (G)
• Experiment with silent conferences.	• Pages 87–91

This week I will provide a parent letter entitled "Program Begins" to send home with each student. Please send it home this Friday.

Thanks!

Sample Parent Letter—Program Begins (2)

To: Parents of (name of school) School Students

From:

Subject: Positive Discipline

We believe that life-long success depends on self-discipline. We have developed a Positive Discipline program that provides students an opportunity to master the skills of self-discipline. We believe that every student needs to take the responsibility for making appropriate decisions about achievement, interactions, safety, and surroundings.

It is our belief and our goal that virtually all of our students will achieve success if we provide adequate instruction and sufficient time for guided and independent practice. Your help is needed with the instruction. A sense of peer support will be developed in the classroom and the school to sustain the growth of Positive Discipline throughout the year.

We will teach students about behaviors expected at school and about making appropriate decisions and choices. Inappropriate decisions and choices will be followed by logical rather than punitive consequences. Students will receive recognitions and awards for growth in Positive Discipline. As these skills are learned, the potential for academic growth is enhanced. We hope you will soon be informed that your child has accepted the responsibility to make appropriate decisions at school that will support growth in Positive Discipline.

We will communicate with you frequently through our school paper and classroom progress reports. Attached is our list of expectations that has been developed by staff, students, and parents. Please review the list with your child and call us with any questions or concerns.

(*Note to Principal:* A list or brochure of all-school expectations, similar to the handouts shared with the staff during the Planning for Implementation phase, needs to be attached to this letter.)

Positive Discipline Bulletin—Week 2 (3)

Teachers and Staff:

Many students are already demonstrating very consistent appropriate behavior! I am enjoying giving praise to students. This week I will include an article in our newsletter called "What's New?" to tell parents about our Positive Discipline program.

This week you have several suggested activities to complete and three new lessons to teach. Remember—if we concentrate on thoroughly teaching behavior now, we will have easy going later.

Teacher Activities

- Review all expectations.
- Provide guided practice for all expectations.
- Continue to build esprit de corps.
- Introduce Classroom Problem Solving.
- Continue to provide recognition for success and logical consequences for inappropriate behavior.
- Discuss the School Team.

Support Materials

- Esprit de Corps Lessons 3, 4, 5 (H, I, J)
- Pages 181–182

Have a super week!

Copyright © 1990 by Allyn and Bacon.

Sample News Article—What's New? (4)

This year we are using a new all-school discipline plan called Positive Discipline. The program is focused on guiding students toward responsibility for their own behavior and toward becoming self-disciplined. We believe they will learn skills that will foster life-long success.

Our expectations (rules) for students are the same as last year. Our approach is different. Through lessons and practice sessions we are teaching students what is expected and how to solve problems appropriately. Students are expected to make appropriate decisions and choices in the areas of achievement, interactions, safety, and surroundings. Wise decisions and choices are followed by positive recognition.

As students demonstrate their growth toward self-discipline they will be invited to join the (*insert school team name here*). Student Council members selected the team name. Students who earn memberships will have special privileges and recognition.

Positive Discipline Bulletin—Week 3 (5)

Teachers and Staff:

This week I will be finalizing the details of our school team. I will probably involve students and staff to get suggestions. I will bring the final plan to you for approval.

It is very important that you review the all-school expectations carefully and do a conscientious job of guiding practice this week. Give lots of positive verbal recognition for appropriate behavior. Maybe you could use a spelling bee or other game format to review the expectations. Be sure that any new students who join your classroom have instruction about the expectations. You may wish to assign a buddy or partner who will help the new student learn how to behave appropriately. This week be sure to plan a short, special activity (see Key Concept 4: Classroom Team Time) for all students who are making progress. Try not to leave anyone out this week. Thank you.

Teacher Activities

- Review all expectations.
- Provide abundant guided practice.
- Provide abundant verbal recognition for success.
- Provide group recognition for progress.
- Provide logical consequences for inappropriate behavior.
- Continue to build esprit de corps.
- Hold a problem-solving session.
- Share new information about the School Team if available.

Support Materials

- Esprit de Corps Lesson 6 (K)

What you expect is what you get!

Sample Certificates and Badges (6)

Certificate
of
Membership

FOR BECOMING A MEMBER OF THE ROYAL
GAMMON KNIGHTS!

Mercedes Pickering, Principal

Certificate
of
Membership

KNOWS ALL THE CLUES FOR BECOMING A
GOLDEN TREASURE TEAM MEMBER!

Judith White, Principal

Sample News Article—New Achievement Group
(7)

Our students have been learning, practicing, and growing in their acceptance of making responsible decisions at school. As a staff we believe that virtually all students can and will master the skills needed to function appropriately in the school community if given adequate instruction, sufficient time to learn, and support.

Since the first day of school, we have been teaching behaviors, expectations, and wise decision making as seriously as math and reading. We have provided guided practice and students are currently practicing independently.

The behavior skills the students are expected to achieve are really life skills. As they practice being in control they are assuming responsibility for their personal achievement, as well as personal safety, respect for rights of others, and caring for our school environment.

During the week of (*insert dates here*) the students currently accepting the responsibilities of good citizenship in our school community will be awarded membership in the (*insert team name here*).

It is our belief that all of our students will achieve success and receive our team award sometime during the year. A sense of positive peer support will be developed in the classroom to continue growth in decision making throughout the year. Additional memberships will be recognized as achievement warrants.

Positive Discipline Bulletin—Week 4 (8)

Teachers and Staff:

I want to compliment each of you! You have done a thorough job of teaching behavior during the first three weeks. This hard work should begin paying off now. Our school team plans are complete and I am anxious to share them with all the students. Please let me know if you would like me to teach the "Introducing Independent Practice" lesson to your class.

Positive Discipline "sponges" are included with the bulletin this week. Sponges are short learning activities that can be used to soak up time (like a sponge) during idle moments. Sponges turn lost time into learning time. The sponges the program suggests are all to be done orally. Feel free to design your own and/or depart from the oral format and use the board, a worksheet, or a transparency.

You will be asking students to do some higher level thinking this week as they analyze and evaluate their own behavior. Select from among the self-analysis charts with this bulletin or feel free to design your own. Again, provide a short classroom Team Time activity to recognize progress this week.

Teacher Activities

- Review expectations by using sponges.
- Teach new lessons.

- Provide recognition including Team Time and logical consequences.
- Continue to build esprit de corps.
- Introduce independent practice.

- Have students complete at least two self-analysis charts during the week.

Support Materials

- Positive Discipline Sponges (L)
- Brain Power (M)
- Staying on Task (N)
- Gossip (O)
- Making Choices (P)

- Esprit de Corps Lesson 7 (Q)
- Introducing Independent Practice (R) and self-analysis charts:
  - Checking Myself
  - Positive Discipline Skills

(continued)

Positive Discipline Bulletin—Week 4 (8) (*continued*)

Teacher Activities

Support Materials

- My Choices Today/This Week
- Student Checklist
- Teacher Checklist

- Diagnose students' progress by reviewing the self-analysis charts to see if you agree with the students or use a teacher checklist.
- Discuss specifics of the School Team.

**Meet me in the lounge right after school today.
I have planned a Team Time activity for us!
You won't need to stay long.**

(*Note to reader:* Some possible staff Team Time activities include serving popcorn and soft drinks after school; providing peppermints and extra chairs so teachers can "put their feet up"; getting together for a brown-bag lunch; providing breakfast rolls, juice, and coffee; serving vegetable sticks and cheese anytime; or providing a large box of chocolates during an after-school get-together.)

Positive Discipline Bulletin—Week 5 (9)

Teachers and Staff:

This week is "catch-up" week or "coast" week, depending on what you have accomplished so far. I am delighted with our progress and I am enjoying giving praise and recognition to so many students. Please share with me the positive feelings and/or concerns you have about our progress in implementing Positive Discipline.

Teacher Activities

- Review expectations by using sponges.
- Provide recognition, including Team Time and logical consequences.
- Provide guided practice and correctives.
- Provide independent practice and extensions for students who are ready.
- Have students complete self-analysis charts bi-weekly or weekly.
- Continue to diagnose student progress.
- Discuss the School Team.

Definition of a genius:
A person who aims at something no one else can see and hits it.

Positive Discipline Bulletin—Week 6 (10)

Teachers and Staff:

The first induction ceremony will be held Friday. Send your new team members to the office anytime between (insert times here). You will not need to accompany them. They are self-disciplined! You will want to reassure those who aren't eligible for membership at this time. Tell them you expect them to become members soon and let them tell you what they will do in order to become eligible for membership. We will have another induction ceremony next week.

Talk more about esprit de corps with all the students and get everyone helping everyone to become members. A classroom team time for all those making progress will help. You may want to inform the parents of students who are not yet ready for club membership. A sample letter is provided with this bulletin. I will mail letters to the parents/guardians of those who do become members.

Teacher Activities

- Review expectations.
- Continue to provide recognition, logical consequences, guided and independent practice, and correctives/extensions.
- Sign certificates for the induction ceremony.
- List students needing more practice (two categories) for the principal.
- Meet with principal/students for support group plans.
- Notify parents of Almost Achievers.

Support Materials

- Sample Letter: Positive Discipline Progress (S)

**This school is a magic place
where together we make tomorrow.**

Copyright © 1990 by Allyn and Bacon.

Sample Parent Letter—Positive Discipline
Achiever (11)

Dear _____

    Congratulations! _____ is successfully demonstrating responsibility for appropriate school behavior and is making appropriate decisions about achievement, interactions, safety, and surroundings. _____ will receive recognition for his or her achievement on _____ at _____, in the _____. You are invited to share in this occasion by attending the ceremony or by recognizing _____'s achievement in your own way at home.

                    _____
                          (Signature)

Sample News Article—School Team Begins (12)

Additional members are being added weekly to our school _____ Team. The total now is nearly _____ (*insert number here*). Students are striving to make good decisions about their behavior. As they assume responsibility for school achievement and effort, playing safely, respecting the rights of others, and caring for our school environment, they are awarded recognition as a member of the _____ Team.

Over _____ (*insert number here*) students have earned membership privileges in our (*insert team name*) Team. The team is a positive way to encourage students to be as self-disciplined as possible. Students who are well-behaved and self-disciplined also make better grades in school. We expect that every student will earn membership this school year. Most students will earn their privileges before the end of the first semester.

If your child has not yet become a member, here's a short checklist to help analyze what needs to be done in order to achieve membership:

3 pts.—Almost Always; 2 pts.—Sometimes; 1 pt.—Not often enough

_____ I am responsible for my own and others' safety.
_____ I am responsible for my own and others' achievement.
_____ I respect myself and others.
_____ I am responsible for our surroundings.
_____ I solve problems appropriately.
_____ Total

(Members of the (*insert team name*) Team consistently earn a total of at least 12 points each week.)

Positive Discipline Bulletin—Week 7 (13)

Teachers and Staff:

 We'll have a second induction ceremony this Friday. Send your new team members to the office anytime between (*insert times here*). As you did last week, reassure those who aren't eligible for membership at this time. Work with them on setting goals for the following week.

 Thanks for all your hard work with our discipline program! I'm interested in hearing how you're feeling about the way things are going.

CHAPTER 9

Keeping All-School Positive Discipline Exciting and Motivating

Once Positive Discipline is in place, it will be necessary to monitor, adjust, and evaluate the program. You will need to accommodate changes that occur after you begin the program, including the arrival of new students and possibly new staff members. Helping everyone adjust as the year progresses will contribute to the program's success. Plan to include a Positive Discipline item frequently on staff meeting agendas during the year in order to afford staff the opportunity to share successful techniques as well as concerns. When problems arise, involve as many people as possible in searching for solutions.

Encourage teachers who have regular small-group meetings to discuss and share successes or failures. Assign a "buddy teacher" to beginning teachers or to teachers who are new to the building. It is beneficial to have a supportive Positive Discipline "buddy" assigned to teachers who recognize they may have problems with the program. Another way to encourage supportive teachers is to organize a Positive Discipline committee. The committee can be selected by the staff as a whole or made up of volunteers, and should meet each week or at least every two weeks. Teachers who are having problems can then meet with the committee. Together they can brainstorm ideas and the teacher with the problem can select one idea to implement. A follow-up meeting with that teacher should be held in one week so progress can be analyzed. If the problem is still not solved, further brainstorming can help.

In this section the authors have included several topics, techniques, and tips that have worked for them during the first year of implementation in their schools. The process of leading a classroom or school community toward the development of self-discipline in students is a continuing challenge and a dynamic opportunity to meet the needs of schools today.

Keeping Positive Discipline Exciting and Motivating for Teachers

The Teacher Who Is a Good Classroom Manager

Year after year, many teachers develop a positive learning environment and good discipline. These teachers would function well without a school plan, but they will enjoy a school where all students and staff are working toward the same goals. They will also enjoy the positive feedback you, as the principal, can provide for excellent classroom management and for the way they relate to students.

For example, you could write a note to the teachers and staff about how much you appreciate their hard work on Positive Discipline. A letter could be mailed to their home. Stickers, pencils, and bookmarks are inexpensive ways to let people on your staff know they make a difference to students. One author kept a teacher "grab bag" filled with free items gleaned at conferences.

The Teacher Who Has a Difficult Class

The wise principal will articulate early in the school year the potential for the Positive Discipline program to make a difficult year easier. It is a challenge for the principal to have an answer or an offer of help ready for the teacher who has a difficult group. It is important for the principal to project confidence and knowledge of the activities available throughout the implementation of Positive Discipline.

The establishment of esprit de corps is especially critical with a difficult class. This sense of "family" creates tremendous peer support for self-discipline. A student, other than one who has serious problems, will indeed find it difficult to hold out against peers, teachers, the principal, and parents. The Support Group will also provide help to the student and the teacher. The fact that help is there often makes the teacher determined to solve the problem alone.

The Teacher Who Says "The Program Does Not Work with My Kids"

A principal's positive approach will help teachers who are critical of the program. No matter how difficult the class or how negative the teacher, you, the principal, can make a difference by being positive about success and by offering the teacher support. One way to offer support is to schedule a conference with the teacher. Begin the conference by getting a clear understanding of what the teacher means by "the program doesn't work." Next, go over the flowchart and the time line to check on what has and has not been done. Explain any points of misunderstanding. At first, the teacher may be unable to believe that virtually every student can succeed. You may need to reinforce the Key Concepts. You will want to assist with ways to help the teacher support every student. You may need to reemphasize the importance of the concept of establishing esprit de corps. If there has been a breakdown at the classroom level, perhaps it may be in this area.

Another way to offer support is in a principal/teacher counseling session. Help the teacher analyze his or her understanding of the implementation of Positive Discipline using the following suggested outline. Jotting down the various responses of the teacher in a brief form may help you both to pinpoint the areas needing more emphasis.

Analysis Outline

1. Review the all-school expectations. Ask which specific expectations seem to be bigger problems than others.
2. Review the classroom expectations. Ask if students were involved in establishing the expectations. Ask which particular expectations seem to be bigger problems than others.
3. Review the Teaching Model. Ask if any parts of the model seem difficult to include. Ask if the teacher tends to leave out any particular steps.
4. Ask what the teacher is doing on a hourly, daily, and weekly basis when students demonstrate appropriate behavior (choose wisely). Is he or she discussing and recognizing appropriate decision making? Discuss what activities are being used for Team Time.
5. Ask for some examples of what the teacher is doing when students demonstrate inappropriate behavior (choose unwisely). Ask about how the students respond to the techniques the teacher is using.
6. Ask how the teacher is feeling about the level of esprit de corps. Ask the teacher to concretely measure the students' feelings of belonging and feeling wanted and needed.
7. Ask for any concrete records of student self-analysis charts. If there are no records, suggest the use of charts for two or three weeks (pages 281–288). Review the results with the teacher.
8. Review the activities being used with any students the teacher has referred to the Support Group.

Help the teacher identify one area as a focus in order to get the program moving again. You may even wish to suggest a time frame for accomplishment. Follow this with supportive observations and emphasize what is going well in the classroom. Offer to reteach some of the behavioral expectations or model giving students verbal positive reinforcement for appropriate behaviors and decision making. This will illustrate to the teacher and students how important Positive Discipline is to you.

Teachers Need Positive Strokes, Too!

The principal can keep the program alive and well for the staff in several important ways. Share positive comments about behavior in the classroom and the building. Share parent comments. Ask teachers to share experiences at staff meetings. Include Positive Discipline frequently as a topic on full-staff agendas. Discuss various school discipline problems as they surface during the year. Refer teachers to the reteaching of appropriate parts of the plan.

After the first weeks of implementation, include a paragraph or two concerning Positive Discipline in each staff bulletin. Sample short paragraphs are included here. Provide opportunities to share and discuss problems. Collectively, seek answers. Take time to write a personal note to a staff member, a class, or a student. Make comments in the school paper about the commitment of the staff on behalf of students.

Sample Staff Notes

1. This week we're having an assembly. Please review the appropriate assembly expectations before coming to the assembly. Frequently (once every hour) talk about and discuss students' appropriate behaviors and their growth in making decisions that are in their own best interest. Give a test.
2. Please review wise decision making, and hall and restroom expectations by using a sponge activity.
3. Please review the lunch room and lunch line expectations. Have students model expected behaviors and have students offer reasons for the need of these expectations.
4. This week, have a problem-solving session and use role playing. For example, the problem could be what to do if someone calls you a name. Emphasize the positive consequences that occur when students choose appropriate reactions to name calling.
5. Now is a good time to increase esprit de corps by having students give each other verbal compliments each day.
6. Please review playground and equipment safety expectations this week. Have students analyze why it is to their benefit to make wise decisions on the playground.

7. By now, classroom Team Time activities may have lost their initial motivational power. Have a brainstorming session with students to get some new activities or check with other teachers to see what other classes are doing. You may want to consider having a classroom team privilege for every day. Make door charts to post so as students enter in the morning they can read the daily privilege. Some examples might include: Monday—skip five math problems; Tuesday—write in ink; Wednesday—get a drink of water whenever you wish; Thursday—draw instead of write in your daily journal; Friday—chew gum all day if you wish.

8. Please review hall and restroom expectations. Connect the review of hall expectations with a review of Fire Drill Procedures in order to highlight the need for making wise decisions about hall behavior.

9. Ask your class to select the expectations they would most like to change and have them state why. Submit suggestions for changes to me.

10. Do you have a special procedure to teach new students the all-school expectations? Plan to share your procedure at the next full staff meeting.

11. Please review playground decisions. Have students think of one new appropriate activity.

12. Please discuss appropriate and inappropriate activities for inside recess. Ask each student to name three constructive things they could do.

13. Please review the all-school expectations. Have a contest.

14. Please review hall, restroom, and assembly expectations. Use a "spelling bee" format. Be sure new and old students know all the expectations.

15. Please review all-school expectations during line-up times. For this week talk about the students' decison-making processes about every half hour.

16. Free week. Do not review expectations.

17. Review the expectations that are most difficult for your students.

18. Do a self-concept building activity and focus on thinking of activities that help others feel OK.

19. Teach a new group game and review playground decisions. Discuss consequences of choices.

20. Have students discuss what it might be like if we had no expectations.

New Staff

A packet of handouts for new staff members will prove helpful and will keep your program intact. An overview of Positive Discipline should be provided and a conference to review written material is suggested. Set your teachers up for success. A little work now will pay big dividends later. For new staff members, the authors suggest the following:

New Staff Packet

A packet of materials for new staff should include:
  pages 21–46
  page 51
  pages 175–186
  pages 241–291

You will be distributing pages 293–311 to all staff after the first seven weeks.

Substitute Teachers

A handout prepared to give to substitute teachers in your building will help sustain the program when teachers are absent. Ask your substitutes to review their experiences at the end of the day. A sample Substitute Review Form is included at the end of this chapter.

The one-day substitute can be an important public relations person in your community. If the individual is impressed with your school and program in one day, he or she will talk about it. For a long-term substitute it is suggested the principal provide an overview of Positive Discipline similar to the packet given to new staff.

Keeping Positive Discipline Exciting and Motivating for Students

Team Members (Achievers)

The team members need some periodic incentives to keep them monitoring and correcting their own decision making. They need to know that they are appreciated and that they are doing a good job. The ages of the students will determine how often incentives need to be provided. Generally, the younger the students, the more frequent the incentive cycle.

Consider an incentive cycle of every three or four weeks for K–6 elementary schools. This should be sufficient because students receive weekly recognition during classroom Team Time and enjoy special privileges almost daily. You may wish to adjust the cycle during certain times of the year. For example, it is a good idea to schedule more frequent team activities during the last weeks of the school year. We have also found it helpful to have a team incentive activity the afternoon prior to a school vacation. A special team activity often channels the restlessness and excitement present at these times.

This list of possible recognition activities and incentives may spark your imagination. Adapt the list to fit the ages of your student population.

- Display names on a hall bulletin board or in the office.
- Provide letters to the family about the success of the student in making good decisions.
- Provide a small concrete reward like a bookmark or a stick of gum.
- Arrange for a special assembly or get-together for team members. Activities could include a sing-a-long, a special speaker or guest, or student performances.
- Provide printed membership cards to carry in wallets.
- Provide printed cards for parents to carry in wallets.
- Arrange for special recognition with teachers, students, and parents when a whole room maintains club membership for a month. This should be a real occasion.
- Teach a school team cheer or chant (see appendix). Students enthusiastically create cheers, chants, and raps. Feature the cheer in an all-school assembly.
- Recognize cultural differences by issuing special letters recognizing appropriate decisions. For example, issue a letter written in Spanish or prior to an important holiday.

Almost Achievers

Even though the classroom teacher is seeing that this group of students is making progress, the principal also needs to relate personally to the group.

After several weeks of effort, this group may profit from small group sessions with the principal. It is suggested these sessions be held periodically. In one author's experience, the increased involvement of the principal brought almost immediate progress.

Several activities might be helpful at these meetings. Congratulations are in order if the students are making improvement. Provide time, for those who are willing, to share behaviors that are no longer a problem for them. Also provide time to share behaviors that are still causing problems. Seek group suggestions. Express that you know the students are trying and that you know they may sometimes be discouraged. Share some of the events in your life that have meant the most to you and that took a great deal of effort.

Most importantly, share your belief in their ultimate achievement. Relate that teachers and principals are human and that everyone occasionally makes poor decisions. Share incidents of your own less-than-great decisions.

Students Working with a Support Group

The principal must maintain contact with the student, classroom teacher, and other support group members. Share the "ups and downs." Support group maintenance need not be time-consuming for the principal.

A brief, private weekly conference or a few words with problem students as you encounter them in the halls or during classroom visits is helpful. Your actions could include any of the following: Encourage students to verbalize what has gone well. Relate positive comments made by the problem student's teacher or support group members. Make contracts to set future goals. Award mini-recognitions for progress. Document progress together. A picture of a staircase may serve to visually show students that reaching any goal is a series of small steps. A simple chart kept in the student's desk or posted just behind the teacher's desk might also be helpful.

New Students Entering the Classroom

Orientation of new students is done primarily in the classroom. The teacher and students inform the newcomer of the expectations and explain the School Team. The advantages of being a member of the team are presented. Since new students usually feel particularly alone when entering a new school, it is helpful to assign a special peer helper. Students most recently succeeding make excellent peer teachers for new students. The new student is then given two to three weeks to practice the expectations. Then, if the student's actions warrant, he or she may be admitted to the team. As an alternative, a new student can be awarded "guest" membership in the team and can receive some privileges as he or she makes progress toward becoming a full team member. Sometimes a review of all the expectations is in order for the entire class. This is a very good way to orient new students. Two review lessons are included in the appendix.

Keeping Positive Discipline Exciting and Motivating for the Community

Parents have been supportive in all the schools that are currently using Positive Discipline. Your community will support the program if you communicate regularly about the progress of your program.

Here are some ideas. Keep the community informed about the percentage of team membership. Comment in the school newspaper about activities. Provide personal letters to parents when a student earns team membership. Contact the local newspaper to suggest a series of Positive Discipline articles. If your area has a monthly neighborhood newspaper, contact the editor. If your school district has a Communications person, he or she is also a helpful resource.

Describe the Positive Discipline program in your parent handbook and further explain the program at parent group meetings. Display team memberships in your office/school. Anything you do with students is carried to the community.

Encourage PTA groups or parent organizations to provide support, money, and/or incentives. Provide parents of Achievers the opportunity to present a library book to the school in honor of their child's achievement. Prepare printed book or game plates that indicate a contribution by an Achiever and that could be pasted in or on games or books. To inform grandparents, aunts, or uncles, encourage team members to "order" a letter from the principal praising a student's efforts at being a good school citizen. The letter can be provided for Grandparent's Day or for inclusion in holiday greetings.

Local organizations, including the Lions Club and the Optimist Club, are interested in speakers. Offer to speak to the group. You may receive additional resources in return for your effort.

Working with Classified Personnel

You will also need to involve playground aides, bus drivers, and other classified staff who work on a day-to-day basis with the students in your school in your Positive Discipline program. The involvement process you use will probably be similar to the one you use with your certified staff. However, this group will most likely need to be taught the basics of Positive Discipline in one short meeting.

The handout at the end of this chapter can be distributed to classified staff and then discussed in sections or in small "job alike" groups. You will then need to continue to follow up with discussions and reteaching as time and need dictates.

Additional Thoughts

We hope you will soon be creating and implementing your own unique Positive Discipline program at your school. It is not possible to emphasize enough the goal of *helping every student be successful.* The principal's belief in and messages about ultimate success are essential. We know you and your staff can be successful. In the near future, you, your teachers, staff, students, and parents will be enjoying the rewards that positive, self-discipline brings.

Sample Elementary School Substitute Review Form

WELCOME TO OUR SCHOOL!

An all-school program, Positive Discipline, is used in our school. Students are responsible for making good decisions about achievement, interactions, surroundings, and safety. We do not expect our students to be perfect, but we do expect them to respond positively if asked to stop a behavior or to do something. As with everyone else, our students like to know they are doing a good job. If you feel they are doing a good job, let them know several times throughout the day.

A folder of pertinent substitute information will be found on your desk. We are pleased to have you in our building and hope you enjoy your work. All staff members are willing to help. Other teachers at each grade level are knowledgeable about procedures in your room.

At the end of the day, please respond to the following:

1. Did you find information and materials adequate for your teaching responsibilities?

2. What could we have done to make your day more pleasant and successful?

3. Any additional comments?

Thank you!

_____   _____
Signature of Substitute   Date

Positive Discipline for Classified Personnel

We are working with a new discipline program called Positive Discipline. Your support is critical to the program's success. Classroom staff members will have the responsibility of teaching our students how we expect them to behave during school time. They will also be teaching students the skills to make wise decisions for their own and others' well being. These skills, when learned, are skills for life-long success. You are being asked to provide positive recognition to students who meet these expectations and make consistently wise and appropriate decisions. You need to talk with students about their decisions. You will need to provide logical, not punitive, consequences to students who do not meet the expectations. More information about logical consequences will be provided. However, you should spend most of your time providing positive recognition. Students need and want attention from adults. Plan to give your attention in positive ways that will help students build skills for life-long success.

Successful students will become members of our school team. You will have a say in whether or not students are eligible for membership. Students on the team will wear a badge and enjoy special school-wide and classroom privileges.

What to Do When Students Choose Wisely

An important part of the Positive Discipline program is recognizing and rewarding students for achieving successfully. As new skills are learned, everyone needs encouragement and praise. Our students are no exception. This is called *providing consistent positive reinforcement.*

Actions to Provide Consistent Positive Reinforcement

1. Establish eye contact and give a silent positive reinforcer such as a wink, a smile, a thumbs-up signal, a sticker, or a stamp.
2. Speak to students who are meeting expectations. For example, "Brian, good job of going down the slide. When you choose to wait until others are not on the slide, it helps keep you and others safe." "Kim, thank you for carefully carrying your tray." "The students in the first four seats are ready for the bus to move."
3. Reward the student or group of students with special privileges. For example, "Students in the back of the bus were so quiet today, they may leave the bus first." "Lisa, you did such a good job of lining up yesterday, you may be first in line today."

(continued)

Positive Discipline for Classified Personnel (*continued*)

Privileges You Can Provide

At Recess
- Lead the line
- Lead a game
- Be first in a game
- Choose the game
- Referee
- Run a race
- Lead the line backwards
- Be the equipment monitor
- Special Friday activity

In the Lunchroom
- Choose own seat
- Sit at a special table
- Sit with a friend
- Stamp on hand
- Certificate or "up" slip
- Display a computer banner
- Help clean table
- Pick up trash
- Help students open things
- Play music

On the Bus (consult the bus supervisor)
- Have gum or candy day (be sure students agree about what to do with trash)
- Lead a song
- Choose own seat
- Certificate of recognition or "up" slip
- Stamp on hand
- Display a computer banner
- Play music

What to Do When Students Choose Unwisely

It is very important to maintain discipline by using every possible positive technique at your disposal. Effective use of specific praise statements directed to students behaving appropriately and making decisions in their own best interest is a powerful tool to stop inappropriate behavior. "Sam is talking quietly" is the statement most likely to get Beth to lower her voice.

(*continued*)

Positive Discipline for Classified Personnel (*continued*)

It is also very important to let students know immediately when misbehavior is not acceptable and will not be tolerated. Generally, you must not ignore or accept misbehavior. The only time it is appropriate to ignore misbehavior is when a student tries a new misbehavior and it is not being reinforced in any way (by other students, for example).

You need a variety of techniques to select from when misbehavior needs to be confronted. First, select techniques that are relatively gentle, kind, and quiet, thereby preserving time, student dignity, and your energy. Here are some suggestions:

1. Address misbehavior in a quiet and relatively kind way:
   a. Get near the student. Walk to where the student is misbehaving and just stand there. This is called *proximity control* and it works in the same way with us when we see a police car on the street.
   b. Use a silent message. Establish eye contact and frown, for example.
   c. Get the student's attention and redirect behavior. For example, call on the student to help with a particular task or answer a question.
2. Address the misbehavior directly and as unobtrusively as possible:
   a. Call the student by name and indicate "no" with a non-verbal signal.
   b. Call the student by name and give a hint or ask a question. For example, "Mark, are you choosing wisely?" "Katie, is what you're doing helpful?" "Melissa, you need to choose more wisely right now."
   c. Direct the student to stop immediately. For example, say in a quiet, gentle yet firm voice, "Sam, stop that, please." "Jane, please no."
3. Address the misbehvior directly and positively.

When misbehavior cannot be corrected by using these techniques, it is time to communicate with the student directly and positively. Use a voice and manner that is friendly and caring rather than controlling and pushy. Stay calm and do not get angry. We need to assume students want to behave and get along. When correction is needed, state the behavior you want in a friendly way.

(*continued*)

Positive Discipline for Classified Personnel (*continued*)

When consequences are called for, select a logical consequence and explain the selection with your normal tone of voice rather than a vindictive or "get even" tone. Examples of typical logical consequences are included. Always allow students to explain, if they wish, but don't accept excuses. Hold students accountable for their behavior. Involve students in solving the problem whenever possible. Always follow these events with positive recognition of the student's appropriate behavior. Do this without fail and as soon as as possible. The intervention will stop misbehavior, but we want also to build self-discipline.

These tyical examples may help clarify the technique of positive, direct communication:

1. State your expectation and state what needs to be done. For example, "Jim, you are not choosing wisely. You are responsible for your behavior. You can do that by sitting down." "Class, you are not all choosing wisely. You are responsible for your behavior. You can do that by lining up quietly." "Carolyn, you are a neat kid, but you are choosing not be responsible for your behavior. I need to hear a quiet voice." Follow up by watching for the desired behaviors and verbally complimenting the student(s) when it occurs.

2. State your expectation. Have the student take some time out to think about choices and behavior. Involve the student in deciding on logical consequences. For example, "Allison, you are responsible for getting along with others. You ran right into Sandy. Take some time out to think about what you can do to show Sandy she is cared for and respected. Tell me your plan when you are ready." Follow up by watching for the desired behaviors and compliment the student when those behaviors occur.

3. State your expectation. Have the student practice and model the expectation. You will be reteaching the expectation and this will need to be done at a time when the student will want to be doing something else. Arrange for the student to lose a preferred activity or lose a privilege. For example, "Julie, I expect you to be responsible for your own safety and the safety of others. You are having a problem with running into others. This is dangerous. You will need to go sit by yourself and make a plan that will help you remember not to run into

(*continued*)

Positive Discipline for Classified Personnel (*continued*)

others. You may not play with others until we discuss your plan." This activity may need to involve the principal. When Julie is allowed to play with the others, follow up by watching for the desired behavior. Be sure to praise her for appropriate behavior as soon as possible.

For "Crisis" Situations

Allow students to cool down. This time may also be needed to let you relax. Hold a private conference. Do not discuss the problem in front of other students. Allow each student to state the problem and how they feel. Insist on a clear statement of what they themselves did, not just what the other person did. Ask, "What did *you* do?" Have each student repeat the other's statement of the problem. Discuss the problem and make a plan for the future together.

Logical Consequences

A logical consequence must be directly related to the behavior it is meant to correct and it must be readily understood by the student. Deliver each consequence with a tone of regret. You expect the student to take control of his or her own behavior by learning to consider choices before acting. If this can be done, you need not take control of the situation.

The following are some examples of logical consequences of student actions.

Examples of Student Actions	*Examples of Logical Consequences*
Shove someone or run into someone.	Have the student take time out to think about the unwise choice and what should be done.
Stand while the bus is moving.	Have the student sit on the bus for a few extra minutes while others leave.
Call someone a name.	Have the student think of and do two things that would help the callee feel better.

(continued)

Positive Discipline for Classified Personnel (*continued*)

Examples of Student Actions	Examples of Logical Consequences
Choose unwisely.	Explain that everyone makes mistakes from time to time. As adults we usually try to correct mistakes or to make up for mistakes. Invite the student to correct the mistake or unwise choice.
Argue about who won or lost game.	Have the student or students take some time to think about how to be a good sport.
Make a mess.	Have the student clean up the mess.
Cut in line or push in line.	Have the student go to the back of the line or move out of the line. The student should line up with you until a verbal plan and commitment to improve is made between the two of you.

The School Team

Once a student becomes a member of the team, membership will not be taken away. It has been earned. However, membership privileges can be temporarily suspended while you and others reteach the student and provide both guided and independent practice. Suspension of privileges should be reserved for the most serious cases of unwise decision making. The decision to suspend privileges must involve the principal. The issuance of a Bus Report will automatically suspend privileges of a team member.

In advance, thank you for your support of the Positive Discipline program. Please don't hesitate to ask for assistance.

**This school is a magic place
where together we make tomorrow!!!**

APPENDIX

Supplementary Materials

This appendix contains handout materials A through S as well as various lesson plans and miscellaneous materials. They are referred to frequently in the text of this book.

Sample Lesson Plan (A):
"Introducing Positive Discipline to Students"

Focus. "How many of you would like to do the very best learning you are capable of, have good friends around you at school, and seldom be in trouble? I believe that all of you can learn to make wise decisions about your behavior at school if I teach you the skills you need, give you the time you need to learn, and support your learning. When you learn the skills you will become a member of our Team."

Rationale. "Today, we are going to begin learning about a program called Positive Discipline. The decision-making skills we will learn will help make this the best school year possible and these skills will help you make wise decisions now and when you grow up."

Objective. The student will state four decision-making areas and give an example of a wise choice in each area with 100 percent accuracy.

Input/Model. "Everyday at school you make many decisions. You decide when to smile at someone. You decide whether or not to keep your desk or locker clean. You decide whether or not to get busy right away at an assignment. You decide whether or not to play safely on the playground equipment or in physical education. You make decisions in four areas: achievement, interactions, safety, and surroundings." (*Note to teacher:* Write these areas on the board. For younger students, the symbols of a book [achievement], two facing stick figures [interaction], a bandage [safety], and a school building [surroundings] can be used to clarify the terms.)

  Discuss the most probable consequence of each decision stated above. Emphasize that wise decisions usually result in pleasant consequences and unwise decisions in unpleasant consequences. Point out that the choice belongs to the student, as does the consequence. Discuss how you will have to sometimes provide logical consequences for students who make unwise decisions. You would rather have students make wise decisions, however.

Guided Practice. Ask students to state examples of possible decisions in each of the four areas. Discuss the consequences of these decisions. Be sure to include some unwise decisions if stu-

(continued)

Sample Lesson Plan (A): (*continued*)

dents do not suggest them so logical consequences can be discussed. Erase the headings for the four areas and have students practice writing or saying the four decision-making areas.

Independent Practice/Diagnostic Progress Check. Have students fold a paper into four sections and label each section appropriately. Instruct them to draw or describe an example of a wise choice and think about the consequences for each choice.

Corrective. Have students who have mastered the objective act as tutors for those who have not mastered the objective. Require only verbal responses for mastery.

Extension. Ask students who have mastered the objective to try to think of a school decision that does not fit in one of the four decision areas. (*Note:* There won't be any.)

Sample Lesson Plan (B):
"Go with the Flow"

Focus. "How many of you have ever taken a trip in a car? What have you noticed about the cars on the highways?" (Answers might include: lots of cars, some go slow, some go fast, sometimes cars pass, there are accidents.)

Rationale. "We need to learn some reasons why it is better when all students walk in the school halls and we don't have accidents."

Objective. The student will walk in the halls of our school, or "Go with the Flow" 100 percent of the time.

Input. "Let's think about one car on a country road. Does the driver need to worry about other traffic? Does the driver need to be careful about his or her speed? Can you think of a time when our halls might be like a country road with just one person on them? When are our hallways like a super highway? Do drivers have to be very careful when there are lots of cars? Do you know what a no passing zone is?" (Explain.)

"It will be very easy to follow the expectation we have to always walk in the halls if you just think about the halls as no passing zones. When you're in a no passing zone, you cannot pass the people in front of you—you 'Go with the Flow.'"

Model/Guided Practice. Suggestions include:

1. As the class moves up and down the hall, the teacher has the children model the objective.
2. The teacher watches the group going to recess or moving through the halls and reinforces the appropriate behavior by giving verbal, specific praise.
3. The teacher gives reminders to "Go with the Flow." When students pass, the teacher supplies the logical consequence, "Pass and you're last."

Independent Practice/Diagnostic Progress Check. Teacher reinforces orderly hall movement as children continue to practice to "Go with the Flow."

(continued)

Sample Lesson Plan (B): (*continued*)

Corrective. Students who fail to "Go with the Flow" are asked to practice during free time or are asked to go to the end of the line ("Pass and you're last").

Extensions. Extensions include:

1. Ask students to think of other examples of activities besides walking in the halls where students help themselves by "Going with the Flow." (One example would be lining up.)
2. Invite students to create additional slogans for "Go with the Flow."

Sample Lesson Plan (C):
"Playground Expectations"

(*Note:* Students need to have prior knowledge of equipment safety.)

Focus. "In about 30 minutes we will be going outside for a practice recess."

Rationale. "Before we can go outside, we will learn about responsible playground behavior and choices so you can play safely and have fun."

Objective. The student will play outside responsibly for 20 minutes with 80% mastery of expectations.

Input. Using a prepared overhead transparency, discuss expectations. For example:

- Choose something constructive to do. (Discuss choices including playing on equipment, running a race, playing a game, etc. Also discuss unwise choices.)
- Agree on game rules first and then play fairly by the rules. (Discuss what happens when this is done and not done.)
- Throw and kick balls, but not rocks, sand, or snow. (Discuss why.)
- When the bell rings, stop playing and walk safely to the building. (Discuss why.)

Model. "What are some things you will see responsible students do outside? Will a responsible student . . . ? What will you do if . . . ?"

Guided Practice. Take the group outside and observe the interactions. Intervene when necessary. Practice the procedure to stop and line up at least twice.

Independent Practice. Observe the interactions and behaviors at noon or during recess when someone else is supervising.

Diagnostic Progress Check. Note problems during these observations.

(*continued*)

Sample Lesson Plan (C): (*continued*)

Corrective. Gather groups with problems together during a supervised recess time and discuss observed problems and appropriate solutions.

Extension. Allow extra play while others are practicing.

Sample Lesson Plan (D):
Esprit de Corps Lesson 1—"Caring for Others"

Focus. "Everyone in this classroom is wanted and cared for by me. You know I like having you in the classroom by the way I greet you in the morning and by the way I smile at you. I show I care for you by helping you with your school work and by listening to you when you tell me things that are important to you."

Rationale. "Each of us can learn how to care for each other. By caring for each other we can create a classroom that everyone wants to come to each day. It will help us want to learn."

Objective. The student will identify three actions that show caring for others when given classroom situations.

Input. Discuss the idea that everyone in the class (not just the teacher) can help all members feel cared for. List appropriate actions or words that indicate caring. Discuss and list situations that help people feel cared for.

Model. Role play with one student using one of the situations listed.

Guided Practice. Have students pair up and choose from the list of situations. Have each pair role play at least one situation and include three apporiate ways to show caring.

Independent Practice/Diagnostic Progress Check. Give three classroom situations and have students write or state three appropriate actions telling or showing how to care for others.

Corrective. Have students make a list of things they remember about last school year that made them feel cared for by others in the classroom.

Extension. Have students think of and/or list TV shows that show caring and tell or write why they think the show contains good examples of caring.

Sample Lesson Plan (E):
Esprit de Corps Lesson 2—"Caring for Others"

Focus. "Have you ever been outside at recess and had to wait and wait to be chosen as a part of a team activity? How did it feel to have to wait? Did you feel cared for by others?"

Rationale. "At some point during every school day each of us wants to feel cared for and special."

Objective. The student will write or state actions that show caring for others.

Input. As a group, discuss actions that make people feel cared for in a classroom. Ask students how they know they are cared for in the classroom. Call attention to teacher actions or words from previous days that demonstrated caring.

Model.

1. Model caring by putting a handmade bookmark in each student's desk. Direct students to examine the bookmarks.
2. Place a small stuffed animal or special pencil on the desk of one student and make a statement modeling caring for that student. The animal or pencil can be kept by the student for an hour or so, then repeat the activity.

Guided Practice.

1. Draw names of secret pals and make bookmarks by writing positive statements and/or drawing friendly pictures. Bookmarks are placed secretly or openly in the secret pal's desk.
2. Pair up students and have them brainstorm ways to show caring. Have each pair choose a favorite way to show others they are cared for and present it to the class.
3. Make and post a list of caring actions.

Independent Practice. Identify practice sessions of ½ day and select new secret pals. Have students select actions from the list that is posted. Whenever opportunities arise, invite students to practice the actions selected. Ten actions can be practiced in one week.

(continued)

Sample Lesson Plan (E): (*continued*)

Diagnostic Progress Check. At the end of each day ask students to list things they have done that showed caring for their secret pal.

Corrective. Have students choose and show someone in the class that he or she is cared for by giving a nonverbal signal such as a wink or a smile, or by sharing materials when appropriate.

Extension. Make a list of ways teachers or students could show others they are cared for in the classroom and give the list to the teacher.

Sample Lesson Plan (F):
"Conflict Resolution"

Focus. "How many of you from time to time have trouble with another student? What are some of the problems you have?" (Someone bumps into you. Someone trips you in a game. Someone calls you a name. Someone won't play by the agreed upon rules. Someone bothers you when you are working.)

Rationale. "You need to know what we expect when problems happen. There are certain things you can do to help solve the problem."

Objective. The student will write or state four conflict resolution strategies with 100 percent accuracy.

Input. Tell the students that their appropriate choices are:

1. Ignore it.
2. Firmly and courteously ask the person to stop.
3. Ask the person to talk it over with you.
4. Report the problem to an adult.

    Discuss the consequences of both wise and unwise choices.

Model/Guided Practice. Role play various problems and choices. Discuss the difference between tattling and reporting. You tattle to get someone else in trouble. You report when you have tried to solve the problem but can't.

Independent Practice/Diagnostic Progress Check. Have students discuss their use of the four choices in conflict situations.

Corrective. Play "What would you do if . . . ?" with a small group that includes students who are good at conflict resolutions.

Extension. Analyze news stories of conflicts and discuss possible appropriate choices.

Special Tip: Some students frequently resort to tattling without attempting to resolve problems. Once you have identified these few students, insist they make a positive statement (tell something they like) about the other student.

Sample Lesson Plan (G):
"Manage Your Fate!"

Focus. "Fighting is not acceptable behavior. If you are in a fight, you are in big trouble and you take a chance of someone getting hurt badly. A fight lasts only a few seconds, but it can take hours or even days to get a fight settled."

Rationale. "If we can identify some of the reasons why students fight, maybe we can find some other ways to handle the problems. I want to help you learn to 'Manage Your Fate!'"

Objective. The student will be able to identify three alternatives to fighting and use them as needed 100 percent of the time.

Input. "It takes two people to fight. Perhaps one person actually starts the fight, but maybe the other person aggravates the situation. Fighting occurs when someone acts in a way that upsets someone else. For example, perhaps you've had a bad morning at home. As you arrive at school, a friend bumps into you. You push back and a fight starts. You weren't really upset with your friend—you were upset by your bad morning at home. Your friend didn't bump into you on purpose. He just wanted to get in the door quickly. Can you think of other situations that might cause a fight?

"Sometimes a fight starts because of an exciting playground game. Someone starts some name calling and someone else gets upset and angry. When you respond to anger or name calling with more anger, you're letting someone else 'manage your fate' or determine what you will do. When you control yourself and decide what to do next, you 'Manage Your Fate.' Sometimes it takes more strength to manage your own fate than to fight. When you decide to control yourself instead of fighting and positively manage your fate, what choices do you have?

"First, you can walk away and think about it. Maybe you really started the whole thing.
"Second, you can tell the other person to stop.
"Third, you can try to talk over the problem with the other person.
"Fourth, you can report the problem to an adult."

(continued)

Sample Lesson Plan (G): (*continued*)

Model/Guided Practice.   Ask students for some examples of situations that can lead to fighting. Role play or discuss the possible solutions and alternatives to fighting. Emphasize controlling or managing their own fate.

Independent Practice/Diagnostic Progress Check.   Pose two realistic situations. Have each student respond on paper with three alternatives to fighting, or call on various students, one at a time, to respond verbally. Ask other students to agree or disagree by using a predetermined hand signal such as thumbs up or thumbs down for agree or disagree.

Corrective.   Role play appropriate solutions to problem situations.

Extension.   Find an example of a typical situation in the newspaper or from a TV show. Discuss solutions and alternatives with a small group.

Sample Lesson Plan (H):
Esprit de Corps Lesson 3—"Including Others"

Focus.   Obtain a puzzle that has as many pieces as there are students in the classroom. Show the puzzle pieces to the class, giving one piece to each student. Indicate that each piece is part of the whole, just like each student is part of the whole class. Have students put the puzzle together. Display the completed puzzle.

Discuss with students what happened while they were putting the puzzle together. Discuss possible alternatives students might have chosen if they did not feel included when they tried to help put the puzzle together (such as: walk away, read a book, put their puzzle piece in their desk).

Rationale.   "Everyone likes to be included. Classrooms are more fun and students learn better when all students feel included."

Objective.   The student will identify and illustrate two actions that include others in play and work.

Input.   Obtain a large piece of mural paper prior to class time. Divide the paper into puzzle pieces equal to the number of students in the class. Do not cut the puzzle into pieces. Show the paper to the class. Tell students that when the puzzle is cut apart, each student will be expected to illustrate actions that include others on their puzzle piece. Discuss that only when each person completes a piece can the puzzle be returned to the whole.

Model.   Begin a list on the board of two or three actions that show others they are included. Illustrate one action. Explain how the actions show that students are included.

Guided Practice.   Over a two-day period have the class add to the list some actions they actually observe that are examples of including others. Once the list has many examples have students select a favorite "including others" action to illustrate. Give each student a puzzle piece (which has now been cut from the whole) and ask them to illustrate their piece with an "including" action. Each student should sign his or her puzzle piece. Reassemble the pieces and display the mural as a whole.

(continued)

Sample Lesson Plan (H): (*continued*)

Independent Practice/Diagnostic Progress Check. Have each student make a five- or six-piece puzzle on regular typing paper entitled "I Include Others." Students may list something they have done to include others on each puzzle piece and illustrate the action if desired. When students complete all their puzzle pieces with appropriate actions, let them glue the sections on additional paper and display them.

Corrective. Just prior to recess ask a student who needs a corrective to select a way to include others in play that day. Ask the student to do the selected activity. Ask for a report after recess.

Extension. Have students bring games from home. Have the class develop sign-up sheets for students to use for the various games and activities available during recess or on rainy or cold days. Have students pair up or choose small groups for indoor recess.

Sample Lesson Plan (I):
Esprit de Corps Lesson 4—"Caring for and Including Others"

Focus. "We all like to feel special. We feel included when someone sits by us. We feel included when someone asks for our help on an assignment. We feel cared for in many ways and enjoy having people support us in a friendly manner."

Rationale. "If we feel cared for and included, it helps us to be excited about coming to school each day and interested in learning at school."

Objective. The student will write or state two reasons why everyone in the class needs to feel cared for and included.

Input. Talk about what was planned for the students by the teacher before school started to develop a feeling of caring and including. For example, the room was attractively decorated, name tags were made, and so on.

Model. Recall things students or teachers have done to help people feel cared for and included in the class and the school.

Guided Practice. Using what was discussed in the modeling, have students practice actions that demonstrate caring and including others.

Independent Practice/Diagnostic Progress Check. In small groups, have each student describe a classroom that would help him or her feel cared for and included.

Corrective. Have students needing correctives act as special "buddies" when students who have been absent return to school.

Extension. Have students make posters using a theme of caring for and including others. Display posters in the halls.

Sample Lesson Plan (J):
Esprit de Corps Lesson 5—"Defining Esprit de Corps"

Focus. "Think of your best friend for a moment. Is your friend in this class? Can you have more than one friend? Can you be friends with everyone?"

Rationale. "When everyone feels cared for and included and works toward group goals, this is called *esprit de corps,* a special group spirit or 'family feeling.' If we learn more about verbal and nonverbal actions demonstrating esprit de corps, we will all become friends and our classroom will be a better place for everyone."

Objective. The student will write or state five actions that show esprit de corps.

Input. Explain that we like to feel included, cared for, and supported by the class group. We like to have friends. When this happens in a group, we say the group has a special spirit or feeling of togetherness and family. The special term for this feeling is a French term, *esprit de corps.*

Model. Invite class members to think of and share instances of how they know they have friends in class. Have the class close their eyes as you describe what the classroom might be like with esprit de corps, or that special family feeling.

Guided Practice. Have small groups practice using verbal and nonverbal esprit de corps actions for situations that have been printed on cards by the teacher. Examples on cards:

1. Robert's crayons just fell off his desk as the art lesson begins. How can you show Robert you are his friend?
2. Leslie doesn't seem to have anyone to pair up with during P. E. What will you do?
3. During lunch Carmen discovers she has lost her belt to her coat. She starts to get worried. What can you do as a friend?
4. Stan seems upset when the teacher hands back his math test. What can you do?

Select actual class situations in order to generate enthusiasm for practicing.

(continued)

Sample Lesson Plan (J): (*continued*)

Independent Practice. Have students write or state esprit de corps actions and practice these actions the remainder of the week, trying to include every class member and beginning to build a feeling of family within the classroom.

Diagnostic Progress Check. At the end of the week have students tell whether or not they feel cared for and included. A secret ballot may be used. With the class, analyze or graph the results and post an esprit de corps chart. Repeat the procedure for several weeks in a row.

Corrective. In small groups, have students continue to practice verbal and nonverbal actions that would show classmates they are wanted as friends.

Extensions.

1. Read students a story that has a theme of friendship and esprit de corps. Have students illustrate or discuss the part that tells about or shows esprit de corps.
2. Provide the beginning of a story that introduces a problem. Have students complete the story using an esprit de corps theme.

Sample Lesson Plan (K):
Esprit de Corps Lesson 6—"Responsibility"

Focus. "What would our room and school be like if everyone followed expectations, made wise decisions, and acted responsibly? What would it be like if we all helped each other act responsibly?"

Rationale. "If we can all learn to help everyone act responsibly and make wise decisions, our classroom and school will be a better place."

Objective. The student will identify three actions that help everyone act responsibly and make wise decisions.

Input/Model/Guided Practice. Discuss techniques students can use to support each other's efforts to make wise decisions and act responsibly. Use actual observed behaviors and gradually involve students in suggesting appropriate supportive actions. Examples include:

Situations	Supportive Actions
Sally picks up some trash from the playground.	Jane says, "Here, Sally, I'll help, too, by putting that in the trash can."
John leaves plenty of space between himself and Sam when he lines up.	Sam says, "Thanks, John, for leaving me some personal space."
Carrie starts to talk to Carlos as they go to music.	Carlos puts a finger to his lips and tells Carrie with a shake of his head not to talk in the halls.
The teacher is ready to start the lesson but everyone is still talking about the recess game.	Joe . . . (Have the students finish this one.)

Independent Practice. At the end of the day have students relate actions they have used to help everyone act responsibly and choose wisely. Repeat the exercise for several days until students easily state supportive actions.

(continued)

Sample Lesson Plan (K): (*continued*)

Diagnostic Progress Check. Have students "grade" themselves on whether they are consistently supporting wise decisions and acting responsibly. Have them give a "thumbs up" signal for support and a "thumbs down" for nonsupport.

Corrective. Invite a guest speaker to talk with students about responsibility and wise decision making. The speaker could be someone from the community such as a lawyer, a high school or college student, or a parent. Have the students prepare questions in advance related to helping people act responsibly.

Extension. Have students write down the word *responsible* in a vertical column and think of a word that shows responsibiliy and/ or wise decision making on the part of students that begins with each letter of the word. For example:

R estroom towels are used and put in the trash.
E rase the boards.
S harpen pencils before the lesson begins.
P ut away materials.
O pen the door for someone.
N oise level should be kept low.
S it at a lunchroom table.
I nteract with others in a friendly, orderly manner.
B ypass looking in other classrooms.
L eave the desk or working area clean.
E xpectations are practiced everyday.

Handout (L):
"Positive Discipline Sponges"

A "sponge" is a short learning activity that can be used during the times of day when learning time is usually lost (lining up, a lesson that ends early, waiting for all students to arrive, etc.). A sponge soaks up this time and converts it into learning time. Sponges can be prepared ahead of time but the easiest ones are verbal. Again, the possibilities are unlimited. Here are a few examples that might stimulate your thinking.

1. Tell students the following story: Rebecca stepped on your toe as she walked by your desk. She didn't say she was sorry or "Excuse me." Which of these three choices is the wisest? Show me with one finger for the first choice, two fingers for the second choice, three fingers for the third choice, and a closed fist for you don't know. Then be ready to tell why your choice is the wisest.

   a. Bump Rebecca's arm as you go by her desk next time. Don't say you are sorry.
   b. Yell, "Ouch!" really loud and disturb the whole class.
   c. Tell Rebecca at recess that you know everyone makes mistakes from time to time and that she just probably made a mistake when she stepped on your toe and did not apologize, but you would feel better if she would apologize.

2. Ask students what they can do when someone calls them a name.
3. Have students name some ways they can show responsibility for safety, achievement, interactions, or surroundings.
4. Pose the following problem for students: You and some friends are playing a game during recess. Someone else comes along and asks to play too. What should you do?
5. Pose the following problem for students: You are going from your classroom to music. The person behind you starts talking to you about something really interesting. What should you do?
6. Pose the following problem for students: You are in the restroom. Someone gets a wet paper towel and says, "I am going to throw this at the ceiling and see if I can get it to stick." What should you do?

(continued)

Handout (L): (*continued*)

7. Pose the following problem: You are outside after school. Someone calls you a name and wants to fight. What should you do?
8. Pose the following problem: Your team just won the game during recess. One person says your team didn't win because the bell rang before your team scored the last point. What should you do?

Sample Lesson Plan (M): "Brain Power"

Focus. "Close your eyes. I'm going to tell you a story and I want you to imagine the story in your head." Tell the story of a school race. Describe the student as coping with an injured knee but still winning the race. Describe the racer as having an attitude that he or she can succeed in spite of the injury. Vividly describe the feelings of a high energy level and active attention.

Rationale. "The racer believed that effort—not luck—ability, and the actions of people determines success. If we believe strongly, our attitude, attention, and energy level can affect our success. We have some control over what we believe about ourselves. We can do anything we set our minds to."

Objective. The student will be able to monitor energy level, attitude, and attention in order to create brain power.

Input/Model. "How do you feel inside when you're getting ready to play a game on the playground? What do you say to yourself? What does your posture look like? If a train goes by, do you pay attention to the train?" Answers will vary. Establish that three factors—energy level, attention, and attitude—help determine success. *Energy level* can be described as excitement or alertness. *Attention* can be described as focus and ignoring other events and thoughts. *Attitude* can be described as thinking "I can!" instead of "Maybe I can," "I can't," or "I don't want to." Also discuss how the factors work when a student is studying a subject that is routine and one that is of interest to the student.

Guided Practice. Teach the following chant using body language (keeping time with feet, clapping, etc.):

> Brain power, brain power,
> The power in me.
> Makes things as easy as one, two, three.
>
> Energy, attention, and attitude,
> Brain power makes me
> One super dude!

After the chant has been learned, distribute the monitoring chart. Practice using the monitoring chart during a classroom

(continued)

Sample Lesson Plan (M): (continued)

game. Stop to tally and discuss energy level, attention, and attitude about every five minutes.

Next, monitor every five minutes during a routine lesson. Note the differences between the two charts. Finally, monitor the routine lesson again as students attempt to increase energy level and attention and improve attitude.

Independent Practice. Have students monitor on their own during regular lessons. Have them choose three times during the day to monitor.

Diagnostic Progress Check. Discuss one of the three monitoring charts with each student.

Corrective. Have students work in groups. Two people should work on a lesson while the third describes energy level, attitude, and attention.

Extension. Identify a difficult task ahead. Monitor the task.

Monitoring Chart

Time	Attention			Attitude			Energy		
				I Can't	Maybe	I Can!			

Sample Lesson Plan (N):
"Staying on Task"

(*Note:* Students need a prior understanding of the term *logical consequences.*)

Focus.   Using a transparency or the chalkboard, show a bicycle. "How many of you like bicycles? How many of you have a bicycle?"

Rationale.   "In order to ride a bicycle, we have to be able to keep our minds on what we are doing. Another way to say this is we need to *stay on task.* In order to do school work, we have to be able to keep our minds on what we are doing—we have to be able to stay on task, too."

Objective.   The student will be able to exhibit on-task behavior while doing school work.

Input.   "Close your eyes for a moment. Think back to a time when you weren't staying on task while riding your bicycle. What happened? What were the consequences? Open your eyes now and tell us." (scraped knee, car honked, people laughed, broke three spokes, etc.). On the chalkboard write:

What Happened	Short-Term Consequences	Long-Term Consequences
Rode in sand.	Scrapped knee.	Couldn't go swimming.
Turned in front of car.	Car honked and scared me.	Was scared to ride the bicycle.
Tried to show off and fell off bike.	Kids laughed.	Felt silly around those kids.

Model.   Erase the board. "Now let's think about times at school when you stay on task during reading or math class":

What Happened	Short-Term Consequences	Long-Term Consequences
Talked with Shelly.	Didn't know what pages to read out loud and kids laughed.	Shelly and I were moved to different parts of the room.

(*continued*)

Sample Lesson Plan (N): (*continued*)

What Happened	Short-Term Consequences	Long-Term Consequences
Fiddled in my desk.	Didn't know assignment and had to ask the teacher to repeat the assignment.	Didn't get finished and had homework to do. Had to use recess to finish.
Read what I wanted to.	Didn't do assignment.	Received a grade of F that day.

Lead a discussion on staying on task and what would have happened in the above examples if the person had stayed on task.

Guided/Independent Practice. Have students select a subject area and practice staying on task for a day, two days in a row, four days in a row, and then an entire week.

Diagnostic Progress Check. Design and duplicate a simple "Staying on Task" record-keeping chart similar to the sample on page 271. Have students record data or record data for students.

Corrective. In a small-group setting, perhaps at recess, have students discuss off-task actions and on-task actions and their consequences. Have the students continue their record keeping and select appropriate positive consequences for an increase in staying on task.

Extension. Have students suggest various positive consequences for staying on task.

Staying on Task

Time	Yes	No

Staying on Task

	Yes	No
Monday		
Tuesday		
Wednesday		
Thursday		
Friday		

Next week my goal is _____

(*Note to teachers:* Be sure you do not question or find fault with the student's negative marks. Concentrate on the positive marks.)

Sample Lesson Plan (O):
"Gossip"

Focus. "There once was a movie about animals. In one part of the movie one of the animals said, 'If you can't say something nice about someone, don't say anything at all.' Perhaps you have heard this phrase before."

Rationale. "You don't feel good about yourself when your friends talk about you in an unkind way. Today we will discuss gossiping and what choices we have in talking about each other."

Objective. The student will practice saying positive remarks rather than negative remarks for a week.

Input. Explain that gossip occurs when people are angry with someone, when we want to hurt someone's feelings, and sometimes when we just want someone's attention. If this happens to one of us, we feel badly and sometimes angry. Then we say things that cause hard feelings. Because of our angry feelings and actions there might be trouble on the bus, in the lunchroom, in the restroom, or outside. Role play situations demonstrating gossiping about one another during telephone conversations.

Model. "Think about some times people have gossiped. I've made a list on the chalkboard. Let's talk about how someone might feel if they hear such remarks." Then ask students to relate positive statements as a way to stop the gossip.

Guided Practice. Have the students team up in groups of three. Give each team three situations on cards. Use the following situations or use some you have overheard without using actual students' names. Have students role play the situations during telephone calls. Students take turns making the calls. Have students discuss after each call how the listener felt who overheard the conversation and what part of the conversation could have been said in a positive way.

> **Christine:** Hi, Jan. You know how dumb Sandy is? Well today I saw her get her science test back. I think I saw an F on her paper. Gee, I knew she was dumb, but, that's really dumb!

(continued)

Sample Lesson Plan (O): (*continued*)

Jim: Hey, Joe, Teddy told me that Kenny weighed in at P.E. and he only weighs fifty pounds. What a runt. He might have beat me out in soccer as goalie, but I bet he gets lots of goals scored off him.

Joe: Wow! I'll start keeping track of all the goals scored off of him.

Sue: Hello, Rhoda. I don't think you should ask Beverly to your party. She's no fun because she never has any tapes. She always borrows mine. Besides, she just wants to be friends with Tammy.

Rhoda: I'm glad you called. I don't want her to borrow my tapes.

Independent Practice/Diagnostic Progress Check. Observe conversation during "relaxed" times, such as waiting for the bus or getting lunches. Note which students are gossiping.

Corrective. Have students who still need practice change the statements on the situation cards to positive statements.

Extension. Students make a list of positive statements that could be used when talking about someone.

Sample Lesson Plan (P):
"Making Choices"

Focus. "Tickets usually tell us we are about to do something enjoyable. They sometimes mean we need to choose things we can do. Think about a time when you were at your favorite amusement park. You bought tickets and then used tickets to go on the rides of your choice."

Rationale. "Here in the classroom you will need to make choices just like you made choices at the amusement park. Making choices that are good for us takes careful thinking. It takes some thinking ahead and some planning. Each week we will have a special Team Time in our classroom. There will be several activities for you to choose to do. Students who are members of the team and those who are making progress toward becoming team members will participate in Team Time. You need to learn to make careful choices about the way you will use the Team Time you earn."

Objective. The student will be able to choose three appropriate activities for and participate successfully in Team Time.

Input. Explain that Team Time is a preplanned time between ten and twenty minutes each week for students to choose special activities. Activities may include art projects with paints or magic markers, puzzles, games, and special small-group projects including skits or listening to tape recorders with headphones. Activities need to vary each week and students need to help decide the activities available for each week. Emphasize Team Time is usually a quiet activity time since some students may need to be doing regular class work. Explain that students will choose only one (occasionally two) activities during Team Time. Students will need to think about the number of minutes they have to get materials out, complete an activity, and then put materials away. They will also need to think about whether or not they wish to include other classmates in the activity and how they can do everything quietly.

Model. Put a list of acceptable activities for a ten-minute Team Time on the board. Ask students to add to the list. Have a student select an activity. Time how long the student takes to get materials out and put them away. Discuss what will need to be considered in order to keep the activity quiet. Repeat the activity with two more students.

(continued)

Sample Lesson Plan (P): (*continued*)

Guided Practice. Divide the class into two groups. One group works on assignments and the other group practices Team Time for ten minutes. Switch group assignments and Team Time activities after ten minutes.

Independent Practice. On a subsequent day, give each students two slips of paper representing tickets to be exchanged for a ten-minute Team Time when assignments are complete. All students should have at least one Team Time during the day.

Diagnostic Progress Check. Observe the interactions after students give you their tickets. Check to see if assignments have been completed. Note and correct any problems that arise during participation in Team Time.

Corrective. Have students observe others using Team Time appropriately. Have them write or draw appropriate choices and behaviors. As soon as possible, allow five minutes of Team Time.

Extension. Give students extra Team Time tickets to use appropriately.

Sample Lesson Plan (Q):
Esprit de Corps Lesson 7—"Working Toward a Classroom Goal"

Focus. "Have you watched TV recently? Think about a show where groups of people were working together."

Rationale. "When everyone pulls or works together, work seems to go easier, goals are met, and rewards are received. Everyone enjoys reaching goals and getting rewards."

Objective. The student will recognize the need for esprit de corps by supporting one another while working toward a classroom goal. Taking part in reaching the goal will show mastery.

Input. Explain that the class will develop a feeling of esprit de corps or family feeling by working together. While the group is working toward common goals, they will feel included and supported in the class. For example, if the class, as a whole, follows all expectations during class time for a day, the class will earn a popcorn party.

Model. Invite the class to think of ways to show esprit de corps to classmates when their classmates don't seem to be following expectations.

Guided Practice. Students practice appropriate actions, including verbal and/or nonverbal actions, which will help one another earn the popcorn party.

Independent Practice. Pairs of students give each other support in following expectations for half a day or for two class periods.

Diagnostic Progress Check. The class, as a whole, has a popcorn party.

Corrective. The class continues to practice for half a day or two class periods.

Extension. Students practice for one week to earn a popcorn party.

Sample Lesson Plan (R):
"Introducing Independent Practice"

Focus. "Students, the last several weeks we have been learning together about Positive Discipline and making wise decisions. Today I want to talk about—now don't laugh—self-cleaning ovens."

Rationale. "Have you ever noticed how your mom cleans a regular oven? She may spray it, or scrub it, or scrape it and finally it may be almost clean. Some of you may have self-cleaning ovens at home. Self-cleaning ovens just clean themselves. No one scrapes or scrubs them. You can be like a self-cleaning oven when you operate by self-control. When you do, things are also easier for you. No one scrapes or scrubs on you."

Objective. The student will understand the analogy of a self-cleaning oven and self-discipline by showing progress toward becoming a member of the school or classroom team.

Input. "We have been learning about Positive Discipline. You have been making decisions about achievement, safety, surroundings, and interactions. We have learned and practiced the expectations and I have guided and corrected you. Now we are ready to begin the time for independent practice. You will operate your own self-control system. When you are self-controlled, you will become a member of our school or classroom team. You will earn privileges—as long as you are self-disciplined."

Discuss the school or classroom team and privileges. Introduce and explain a self-analysis chart similar to those provided on pages 281–288. Explain to students that analyzing their own behavior will help them know in what areas their self-direction is working.

Model. Using a transparency and an overhead projector, demonstrate how to mark the chart you have selected from those provided on pages 281–288.

Guided Practice. Have students analyze their behavior chart for the week. Explain you will need to agree with their analysis.

Independent Practice/Diagnostic Progress Check. Provide a chart at the end of each subsequent week. Gradually withdraw the

(continued)

Sample Lesson Plan (R): (*continued*)

requirement for teacher agreement as students become realistic about their self-analysis.

Corrective. After one week have students focus on just the areas that need correction. Have students ask friends to help with reminders in problem areas.

Extension. Have students develop a self-analysis checklist for use at home.

Self-Analysis Chart:
Positive Discipline Skills

POSITIVE DISCIPLINE SKILLS

3 = almost always; 2 = some of the time; 1 = not often enough

CHECKING MYSELF

	Monday	Tuesday	Wednesday	Thursday	Friday
Achievement					
Interactions					
Safety					
Surroundings					
TOTALS:					

Next week my goal is to: Weekly Total_____/60

POSITIVE DISCIPLINE SKILLS

3 = almost always; 2 = some of the time; 1 = not often enough

CHECKING MYSELF

	Monday	Tuesday	Wednesday	Thursday	Friday
Achievement					
Interactions					
Safety					
Surroundings					
TOTALS:					

Next week my goal is to: Weekly Total_____/60

Self-Analysis Chart:
My Choices Today/This Week

POSITIVE DISCIPLINE

My Choices Today

Achievement ◯

Interactions ◯

Surroundings ◯

Safety ◯

POSITIVE DISCIPLINE

My Choices This Week

	Monday	Tuesday	Wednesday	Thursday	Friday
Achievement	◯	◯	◯	◯	◯
Interactions	◯	◯	◯	◯	◯
Surroundings	◯	◯	◯	◯	◯
Safety	◯	◯	◯	◯	◯

Self-Analysis Chart:
Thinking About Me: An Assessment of Personal Worth

1. I like me because . . .

2. I can . . .

3. I love to . . .

4. I'm afraid when . . .

5. When I grow up . . .

6. I'm learning to . . .

7. I hate . . .

8. Kids seem to like me when I . . .

9. I'm sorry when . . .

10. I'll be happy when . . .

(over)

(*Notes to the teacher:* Were all questions answered? Do the answers indicate love, hate, fear, trust? Star the two answers that seem significant. Give the self-study again in three weeks and in three months. Has the student made progress? Discuss the results with the school counselor or psychologist for further interpretation of results.)

Sample Self-Analysis Student Checklist

Student's Name _____ Room _____

3—Almost Always
2—Frequently
1—Occasionally
0—No Progress

3	2	1	0	Expectations
____	____	____	____	I obey adults.
____	____	____	____	I leave personal space.
____	____	____	____	I move with the traffic flow.
____	____	____	____	I respect others and try to treat them the way I like to be treated.
____	____	____	____	I fulfill safety expectations on the grounds and when playing.
____	____	____	____	I walk single file on the stairs. (Exception: Fire and Tornado Drills)
____	____	____	____	I walk to school and cross streets properly.
____	____	____	____	I obey the bus driver.
____	____	____	____	I fulfill the bicycle expectations.
____	____	____	____	I know expectations for students in the library and I fulfill them.
____	____	____	____	I fulfill expectations provided by the physical education teacher.
____	____	____	____	I fulfill expectations provided by the vocal music teacher.
____	____	____	____	I accept correction well.
____	____	____	____	I have a good attitude.

(continued)

Sample Self-Analysis Student Checklist (*continued*)

3	2	1	0	Classroom Expectations (List your classroom expectations.)
—	—	—	—	_____
—	—	—	—	_____
—	—	—	—	_____
—	—	—	—	_____
—	—	—	—	_____

Sample Teacher's Checklist

Teacher's Name _____ Room _____

Student's Name _____

3—Almost Always
2—Frequently
1—Occasionally
0—No Progress

3	2	1	0	Expectations
____	____	____	____	Student obeys adults.
____	____	____	____	Student leaves personal space.
____	____	____	____	Student moves with the traffic flow.
____	____	____	____	Student respects others and tries to treat them the way he or she would like to be treated.
____	____	____	____	Student fulfills safety expectations on the grounds and when playing.
____	____	____	____	Student walks to school and crosses streets properly.
____	____	____	____	Student obeys the bus driver.
____	____	____	____	Student fulfills the bicycle expectations.
____	____	____	____	Student fulfills expectations for students in the library.
____	____	____	____	Student fulfills expectations provided by the physical education teacher.
____	____	____	____	Student fulfills expectations provided by vocal music teacher.
____	____	____	____	Student accepts correction well.
____	____	____	____	Student has a good attitude.

(continued)

Sample Teacher's Checklist (*continued*)

3	2	1	0	Classroom Expectations
				(List your classroom expectations.)
——	——	——	——	——————————
——	——	——	——	——————————
——	——	——	——	——————————
——	——	——	——	——————————
——	——	——	——	——————————

Handout (S):
Positive Discipline Progress Letter

To:

From:

Subject: Progress in Positive Discipline

    Several weeks ago you received our staff letter about our school Positive Discipline plan. We are happy to report that _____ is making progress toward our school goals. The checklist below shows areas of growth and progress and also areas where additional growth is needed.

    As you can see, progress is being made and we feel the growth needed for becoming a Positive Discipline Achiever will soon be met.

	Is Achieving	*Is Making Progress*
Achievement	_____	_____
Interactions	_____	_____
Safety	_____	_____
Surroundings	_____	_____
Comments:		

_____

_____

Review Lesson: "Expectations"

Focus. "If I told you we were going to have a pop quiz over our expectations, how many of you would do well on the quiz?"

Rationale. "It is hard to remember and fulfill all the expectations just like it's hard to remember everything in a chapter of our social studies book. To keep our knowledge fresh, we have to review before we take a test.

"Knowing and fulfilling expectations is a little like taking a test everyday. Sometimes you remember and fulfill the expectations and other times it's hard to remember. Expectations are needed so all students have the same opportunity to learn."

Objective. The student will fulfill expectations on a daily basis.

Input/Model. Name the four expectation areas: achievement, interactions, safety, and surroundings. Name one or two expectations and the area where they fit. Ask students to name other expectations and areas where they fit. Next, ask students what would happen if there were no expectations for the school or classroom. Have them name the areas where problems would occur.

Guided Practice. State each expectation and have students verbally categorize each one in one of the four areas that are written on the chalkboard. Then state areas and have students respond with expectations in that category.

Independent Practice. Students practice fulfilling expectations during their daily school routine.

Diagnostic Practice Check. Observe students and note which students need a corrective in a certain area to fulfill expectations.

Corrective. Students meet with teacher and discuss fulfilling expectations.

Extension. Have students acknowledge other students when they fulfill expectations.

Review Lesson:
"Reestablish Esprit de Corps"

Focus. Relate a recent incident during which a student or students created a problem in the class or in the halls. Do not use students' names.

Rationale. "If we review and discuss the feeling of group support or esprit de corps, our classroom will be a better place in which to learn."

Objective. The student will be able to recite or write the meaning of esprit de corps and give one classroom and hall example.

Input/Model. Lead a discussion on esprit de corps. Begin by reminding students that we all like to feel included, cared for, and supported by the classroom group. We all like to have friends. Ask for examples of actions that have contributed to esprit de corps or a feeling of including, caring for, and supporting one another. On the chalkboard write the title, "Actions." Caution the students that students' names are not to be used during the discussion. Invite students to name an esprit de corps action they have observed in the classroom or in the hall. List those actions. Continue to discuss the feelings that come from the knowledge and practice of esprit de corps.

Guided Practice. On a 3 × 5 card have each student draw a thumb. After a few minutes of drawing, explain that the thumbs will be used to show whether or not the actions listed build esprit de corps. Thumbs up will mean the action builds esprit de corps, thumbs down means the action does not contribute to esprit de corps. The teacher will tally the numbers of thumbs up and/or down for each action listed on the chalkboard.

    The teacher states each action and says, "Show me." Students are to hold thumbs up or down depending on how they wish to vote. Monitor for any signs of strong feelings felt by individual students. Encourage students to share their feelings with the class.

Independent Practice. Have the students illustrate a class and hall showing people performing actions that build esprit de corps. Have students write the meaning of esprit de corps on the picture. Display the work in the room and/or in the hall.

(continued)

Review Lesson: (*continued*)

Diagnostic Progress Check.   Observe how students are treating one another during the school day. Note which students need more review and practice.

Corrective.   Construct or have students make a one-week log or journal entitled "Ways I Show Esprit de Corps." Each day, allow students five to ten minutes to draw or write about their actions. Be sure students understand you will look at their logs and visit with them or write comments in the logs each day or at the end of the week depending on your schedule.

Extension.   Separate students into four or five groups and have them choose a chairperson. Ask the groups to imagine what might happen if everyone in the world would demonstrate esprit de corps. After five minutes, call the groups back and have each chairperson report on the small-group discussion.

Sample Lesson Plan:
Esprit de Corps—"Helping Others Feel Worthwhile"

Focus. Read a newspaper clipping about the current problem of drug use. Choose an article about your own community.

Rationale. "When people feel worthwhile, they are less likely to use and/or abuse drugs. If we help everyone in our class feel worthwhile, we will all be less likely to need to use drugs."

Objective. The student will learn to exchange positive statements about one another.

Input/Model. "Everyone knows drugs are bad for us. The newspapers and television often tell of drug abuse problems in our community." Have students give information about problems they've heard or read about. Discuss making statements that help others feel worthwhile. Encourage statements that describe the actions of others. For example, "I think Joe is worthwhile because he helped me with a math problem." Start by making statements about four or five students.

Guided Practice. Distribute large pieces of construction paper and ask each student to create a border and leave room for other students to write positive statements about worthwhile actions. Give students the opportunity to write positive comments on each paper. Laminate these creations and return them to each student.

Independent Practice/Diagnostic Progress Check. Provide opportunities for students to give each other positive statements. Observe when statements are being made during unscheduled times.

Corrective. Have students make at least two positive statements about themselves.

Extension. Have students lead a small group in exchanging positive statements.

Copyright © 1990 by Allyn and Bacon.

Sample Lesson Plan for Older Students: "Gum Chewing"

Focus. Hold up a package of gum. Ask why gum chewing can be a problem in class.

Rationale. "It would really be pleasant if we could allow gum chewing more often. We can, if we agree on the solutions to problems gum chewing can cause."

Objective. The students will be able to state potential problems with gum chewing and arrive at solutions.

Input. "Chewing gum in our class is okay if students use appropriate judgment concerning potential problems. For example, gum wrappers need to be disposed of appropriately and gum-chewing noises must not interfere with our lessons."

Model/Guided Practice. Ask students to list potential problems with gum chewing and their solutions. Write the list on the board. You may also wish to discuss and agree on reteaching methods and logical consequences to use if gum is not used appropriately. Allow gum chewing at designated times only. Verbally recognize students who are using gum appropriately. Follow through with reteaching/logical consequences.

Diagnostic Progress Check. Allow gum chewing only in the morning. Observe and record data. Involve students in observing one another and discuss the results in a class meeting.

Corrective. Schedule a private meeting using a classroom leader as a peer teacher. Ask for a report of the meeting.

Extension. Have students present a plan to the principal or student council which allows more flexibility in gum chewing than is currently accepted in the school.

Sample Lesson Plan:
"Analyzing Esprit de Corps"

Focus. Sometimes teachers and students can get discouraged about what is happening in the class. Teachers can feel they aren't doing a great job because of discipline problems. Nearly all students have some negative feelings about their classmates or themselves.

Rationale. "If we realize others, even teachers, get discouraged and have less than positive feelings sometimes, it helps all of us to work toward having positive feelings and toward increasing esprit de corps. It also helps when we express those negative feelings in appropriate ways."

Objective. The students will write one paragraph about their own feelings of classroom esprit de corps.

Input/Model. Talk about your own positive and negative feelings of esprit de corps by describing two or three actual classroom incidents from the past month. Do not use students' names.

Guided Practice. Ask students to volunteer to describe one positive and one negative feeling of classroom esprit de corps without using students' names.

Independent Practice/Diagnostic Progress Check. Engage the class (and yourself) in spending ten minutes in writing about feelings of esprit de corps. Announce you will read everyone's writing and you may schedule conferences with some students.

Corrective. After you've read the results of the assignment, meet with students to discuss feelings expressed.

Extension. Have students write about other positive and negative feelings.

Sample Lesson Plan for Older Students:
"Expectations"

Focus. "Students are willing to follow reasonable or fair expectations. We are here primarily to learn, but it is also important for everyone to feel comfortable and to enjoy being in the class. Teachers need to have "order" in the class so all can learn. You need to have the opportunity to learn and everyone needs to feel safe. Teachers are anxious to share the lessons and help you get to work. Sometimes adults take it for granted that you know how you are expected to behave. The way a student chooses to behave in class affects not only that student's learning but usually everyone else's learning."

Rationale. "Since you are going to be expected to know and fulfill expectations for this class, we will decide together what the expectations will be this year."

Objective. Students will assist in determining classroom expectations.

Input/Model. Write or have written on the board some typical classroom expectations. Have the students read, discuss, and add to the list. Some typical statements might include:

1. Raise hand for permission to speak or get out of seat.
2. Bring supplies (books, pencils, paper) to class.
3. Hang coat on the back of your chair.
4. Remain in your seat until dismissed.

Guided Practice/Independent Practice. Involve students in determining the expectations for the class. Students need to discuss why the suggested expectations will or will not work for them. You may wish to appoint a discussion leader and/or have students vote on classroom expectations.

Diagnostic Progress Check. Observe student input and reactions as you guide the discussion.

Corrective. Have students write about why certain expectations will or will not work for them. Encourage them to suggest expectations that will work for them. Allow them to present their alternative expectations to the class for discussion and/or a vote.

Extension. Have students design posters listing the class expectations.

Keeping Positive Discipline Exciting and Motivating: Maintenance Sponges

Expectations

At the end of an assigned paper, ask students to write down the names of three classmates who are fulfilling classroom expectations.

Esprit de Corps

Encourage students to write "good news" notes to the parents of classmates who have been demonstrating positive contributions to esprit de corps.

Say, "We are looking for positive actions that contribute to classroom esprit de corps. How do you feel when someone names you and something you have contributed?" Encourage a short discussion. Ask students to write down one positive action for each member of the class.

Choices

Have students list five people in the class they would hire if they were an employer. Discuss characteristics of people who get and hold jobs.

Problem Solving

Say, "Someone calls you a name. What do you feel is a response that will help solve the problem?"

Problem-Solving Session: Disruptive Behaviors in the Classroom

Focus

Just after a disruptive classroom incident, ask students to clear their desks, leaving only a piece of paper and a pencil. Give a two-minute assignment: Ask students to draw or write about what they saw and heard.

Group Discussion

Have students sit in a circle or semi-circle. Begin the discussion by asking various questions:

Who was involved in the disruption?
What did they say?
What do you think was the cause of the conflict?
What else could have been said or done?
How do you think the people involved feel?
As a bystander, how do you feel?
Could the classroom disruption been resolved peacefully?

Problem-Solving Objective

Ask students to suggest various ways people can help peacefully resolve conflicts. Some answers may be to share, laugh and go on, take turns, ask an adult for assistance, flip a coin, draw straws, or apologize. If an apology is mentioned, clarify by explaining that an apology doesn't necessarily mean you're wrong, it may mean you are just really sorry about the situation.

Problem-Solving Objective

Ask students to discuss note passing. Clarify when note passing is a problem and when it is acceptable. Ask for consensus agreement on note passing in your classroom, reteaching possibilities, and logical consequences.

Problem-Solving Objective

Discuss getting homework done and returned to class. Stress the need for independent practice on some skills and the increased opportunities for learning. Discuss reasons for not getting homework done. Ask for consensus agreement on reteaching strategies and logical consequences.

Problem-Solving Session: Playground Conflicts

Focus

Draw pictures on the blackboard of an octopus, a worm, a blowfish, an elephant, a hippo with a wide open mouth, a squirrel gathering nuts, and a roaring lion. Caution students to not mention names during the discussion.

Group Discussion

Begin the discussion by saying, "What people actions do you think of when you look at this octopus?" Write responses on the board under the octopus. Responses may vary:

1. He's always in the middle of things.
2. He always has a hand on the ball.

Next ask, "What are some ways to deal with the octopus? What could you do?" Record some of the responses.

Next ask, "In what ways can the octopus act positively on the playground?" Responses may vary:

1. Since he's so good and fast, he could pass the ball around.
2. He could keep his hands to himself.
3. He could try not to choke people.

Then, ask, "Now would the octopus be more fun to play with? Would he be more welcome in a game?"

Proceed to discuss each animal. During the discussion, the behaviors that are causing real problems will surface. You could initiate a series of problem-solving sessions by beginning each with a statement like. "You know, today on the playground I saw a tiger."

Keeping Positive Discipline Exciting and Motivating:
Team Chants, Cheers, and Raps

You may have some cheers, chants, or raps you already use in your classroom or school. Adapt them for your Positive Discipline Team. You might wish to call a local cheerleader for additional materials to adapt. Your best source for material is your own students. Appoint a group of yell leaders and have them develop a chant, cheer, and/or rap for the team. Students really enjoy developing material, performing, and participating.

Sample Cheer—Cool Cats Cheer

We're the Gammon Knights, we're real cool cats.
We make wise decisions 'cause that's where it's at!

Refrain: (Use actions)
Hands up, wise decisons, wise decisions,
Hands down, wise decisions, wise decisions.
Hands right, wise decisions, wise decisions.
Hands left, wise decisions, wise decisions.

Let's all be Gammon Knights, be real cool cats.
Let's all make wise decisions, 'cause that's where it's at.

Refrain:
Hands up. . . .

Sample Rap

We're the Golden Treasure Team, we're proud and fine.
We're the baddest ones you see all the time.
We're bad, oh yeh.
We're bad, we're cool.
We're the baddest ones in this whole school.

Working with Problem Students

As you work to pinpoint specific behaviors that are causing a problem student the most difficulty, it is helpful to use some type of checklist. Two of the authors have successfully used the following:

Weekly Checklist of Problem Behaviors

Week of _____   Student _____

		M	T	W	Th	F	Comments
Refuses reasonable request even when request is repeated	am / pm						
Talks to self	am / pm						
Argues with teacher	am / pm						
Excessive noise	am / pm						
Excessive movement	am / pm						
Wanders	am / pm						
Physical complaint	am / pm						
Angry/explosion	am / pm						
Withdraws or sleeps/lies down	am / pm						
Cries	am / pm						
Throws/drops things	am / pm						
Destroys property (own or others)	am / pm						
Problem with other student	am / pm						
Focuses on fear or worry	am / pm						
Acts tired/sleepy	am / pm						

Positive Discipline—After the First Year

The Positive Discipline program you design will work even more successfully as teachers and students grow in the area of quality decision making. As you begin each succeeding year of implementation, ask yourself or your group several questions:

1. What aspects do we want to keep because they really worked well? What do we want to delete or change?
2. Do we start completely over again, or do we need to change minor parts of our plan? Some of our students who have struggled will struggle again. Could we provide more time and/or support another way?
3. Do we keep the same expectations? (Chances are you will want fewer expectations.)
4. What were the problems? Is there help for resolving those problems already in the program? Do we need to develop additional materials?

What will emerge is a better program for your unique school.

How Analysis and Change Works

For one of the authors the program began to have serious problems when spring fever arrived with warm weather. We began to see more fighting, more disruptive behavior in classrooms, and general unrest on the playground. Careful analysis showed most of the problems involved less than 5 percent of the total enrollment and involved primarily fifth- and sixth-grade students.

Our next step was to analyze staff behaviors. Teachers were not consistently using recommended techniques. We found 20 percent of the fifth- and sixth-grade population were new students. For example, teachers had not asked new students to analyze behavior on a weekly basis and set goals. The principal had been less than supportive in providing teachers and pupils with positive recognition and students wanted more privileges.

Several changes were discussed and implemented. First, room and school expectations were reviewed for three days. Teachers agreed to be more careful about being on duty to monitor and provide positive interactions. We agreed on more privileges and issued daily "tickets" that could be accumulated for small, concrete items or special privileges, including an agreement to exchange twenty "tickets" for lunch with the principal.

At the end of three weeks, 98 percent of the fifth- and sixth-

(continued)

Positive Discipline—After the First Year (*continued*)

grade students were again making consistently wise decisions. A positive message had been sent: Quality decision making affects the quality of your daily life.

Almost any discipline plan will work if it is consistently implemented. If and when problems occur with your program, you need to reread and study this guide. Support the staff and/or students by recognizing what they are doing well and provide leadership in analysis and problem solving. A form is located on page 317.

You make the difference. You must never waver in your belief that your school plan can provide practice in life skills for all students. Positive Discipline will not completely eliminate the problem of students who cause you to turn gray or pull out your hair. Positive Discipline will help students to improve and will support a friendly school climate in which students and staff can work and be together.

Problem Analysis

Directions: Keep a record of problem situations for three days.

	Observed Problem	Observed Problem	Observed Problem
Who?			
When?			
Where?			
What?			

1. List students involved in more than one incident.
2. Is one particular time of the school day more of a problem than other times?
3. List students who resolved conflicts peacefully.
4. What can I do to help students solve their problems? (Brainstorming with others may help.)
5. What skills do I need to teach to help students resolve conflicts peacefully?

Index